D0295739

Whisk(e)y

Örjan Westerlund

Whisk(e)y

HISTORY, MANUFACTURE, AND ENJOYMENT

SOUTH DUBLIN COUNTY LIBRARIES	
SD900000114585	
Bertrams	31/10/2013
	£12.99
	HA

*h.f.*ullmann

Contents

Foreword —masses of history!

Writing a book about whisky becomes more and more of a challenge. You need to be innovative and discover areas for your readers that have never been researched, blowing life into the embers. It's entirely possible to be innovative, but where it's a case of historical accounts, as it is here, there's more scope for creativity in the presentation than in the hard facts. So, Jasper Newton remains Jack, and John is still called Johnnie.

By way of introduction, there is a long and, in places, in-depth section on the history of whisky, much of it about Scotland. It's here that we see the beginnings of the aura that surrounds our favorite drink; monks, smugglers, illegal distilleries and expansionary export entrepreneurs. The section is based on both interviews and study of the literature. I hope you'll enjoy the appetizing details I've included of both events and characters. Following that, there are chapters on a number of major whisky-pro-ducing countries, with their angle on the history, and also sections on newcomers on the whisky scene and, lastly, on production and, briefly, on sensory analysis. Hopefully, the book will arouse and deepen your interest in whisky. Once again, my starting point is the only thing I can rely on in this context, at least while writing, i.e. I've confined myself quite simply to writing what I myself would be interested in reading about.

For the most part, the book is about all the most fascinat-ing aspects of whisky; all the history and the anecdotes which are, and continue to be, the basis of interest in this drink. So, at this point towards the end of the introduc-tion, I'd like to refer you to a short passage from Robert Lewis Taylor's *'Winston Churchill: An Informal Study of Greatness'* (not wishing to make any comparisons, other than to say that the muse of whisky sometimes wafts past when you're least expecting it):

"You must have put in an enormous amount of work on this," commented a newspaper editor who was going through a manuscript with Churchill.

"Yes," replied Churchill. *"And whilst doing so I have con-sumed a greater amount of whisky than perhaps anyone else in the world!"*

So—is the text that follows the outcome of a huge amount of work or is it simply the result of drinking unrivaled quantities of whisky? That's something for you to decide. I do wish you, however, the pleasure of a good snifter while you're reading and sincerely hope that it will be an entertaining experience.

The author, Stockholm, with a warming glass of Bruichladdich Infinity in his hand.

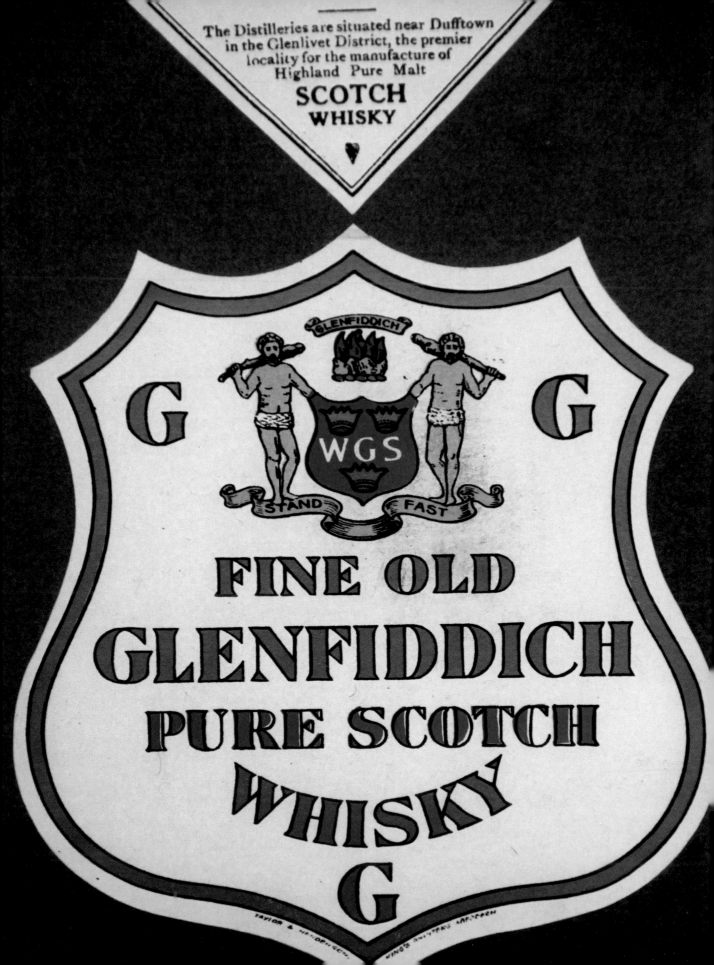

History of Scottish whisky and how it all started

A widely-traveled global citizen with experience and charm

This is the story of a global citizen who has experienced both adversity and fabulous successes. This citizen that we are so familiar with, i.e. whisky, is of course just one drink among many; the difference, however, is that the image of whisky has been built up more carefully, and has largely been fashioned through a conscious marketing effort, mainly through what is now called storytelling.

Alongside the creative efforts of marketing departments stands the image that we as whisky drinkers construct; on the one hand sparkling brooks and deep voice-overs, on the other a dram and a moan of sensuous pleasure. Our everyday whisky is the unassuming glass after a November walk, the few sips taken while cooking on a Friday evening, or in a cognac glass after Christmas dinner. This is a whisky that is consumed, a whisky that's an integral part of our lives and which creates an image of the drink alongside the images of advertising.

For me, whisky is a buddy who has been around the world. He's starting to get on in years and has put on some weight—more, for sure, than a slimline grappa or a new-born vodka trend. He has a personality that we can only get to know gradually; he's someone with rich memories, callous hands, and a whole lot of experience under his belt. A good part of this fascination for whisky is based on its history and on the cultural elements that have been passed down generations, liberally spiced with incredible stories, sentimental family memories, a romantic view of nature and some surly Scots ready for attack, with axe and kilt. Scotland and whisky are intertwined. Like

a golden stripe in tartan, the development of whisky has followed developments in society, from economic self-sufficiency to industrialization and international dissemination. For us whisky drinkers, it's the history that makes the difference between whisky and other liquor. It's history that lends whisky its richness, balance, and a wonderful long-lasting aftertaste—and leaves us wanting more.

In the beginning—the fifth element

Distillation is a process dating back thousands of years. Its history includes the attempts of the Egyptians to separate the four elements, the Mesopotamians who produced perfume using distillation, and later also the Indians who were distilling arrack as early as 800 BC. There are many contenders for the honor of having been the first to produce liquor. There was knowledge of distillation, practical or otherwise, in ancient times even if it didn't at that stage involve distillation of alcoholic drinks.

I should make it clear at this point that the identity of the first person to distill alcohol is lost in a cloud of alcohol vapor. According to some sources, the Arabs were already able to produce liquor distilled from wine

by the start of our calendar system. Distillation as such, and the word *destillare*, a Latin verb that means drop or trickle down, can be found as early as the 2nd century AD in a description by a Roman writer of how to extract turpentine from resin. Likewise, there are medical records from Greece in the 5th century showing how medicines were extracted as condensate from the steam produced from boiling a rather unappetizing mixture of water, lime, and sulfur.

The origins of distillation itself are also unclear and it's quite possible that the knowledge may have arisen in several places at the same time. The Chinese are usually credited with various inventions such as spaghetti, paper and gunpowder, and at least for the latter there's an association with liquor as alcohol had a role in the manufacturing process. It is, however, not known whether either European or Byzantine alchemists had acquired proficiency in distillation before the Chinese. It may be the case, even if it is not documented. When it comes to distillation of ethanol,

however, it has been established that the Russians learned from the Chinese. Regardless of where the knowledge came from, it was the Russians who took a major step towards making alcohol widely available when they discovered that distilled wine could be replaced by a much cheaper wash based on grain.

To begin with, the history of whisky coincides with the history of liquor. One isolated romantic ascribes to the Vikings the honor of having taught people in our northerly parts how to distill. The theory is that these seafarers, travelling to the east for trade and cultural exchange, brought knowledge about distillation home with them from what is now Turkey and the Middle East; a flattering notion, perhaps, for that gang of brutes often depicted as sword-wielding eaters of fly agaric toadstools, clad in bearskins and looking dark and bloodthirsty.

There is a more established idea about how we Europeans learned the mysteries of distillation which

is similar to the above; it also has its origins in the Middle East, although with the involvement of Christianity. Here too the force of arms plays a role, through the Crusades, and there was also input from more peaceful pilgrims on their way to the Holy Land.

If it is the Crusades that we have to thank for our knowledge of distillation, distilled wine couldn't have existed in Europe until sometime around the 12th century. That also tallies well with the fact that the Moors in Spain, despite their presence there earlier, contributed to developments by inventing and distributing the pot still, or alembic, which remains to this day the principal method of distilling batches of aromatic liquor, e.g. cognac, calvados and similarly also whisky. It's easy to see how this could lead to doubt amongst those of orthodox faith, since the Prophet did after all advocate abstinence from alcohol. It can therefore be assumed that the Moors used their knowledge to provide medical prescriptions rather than for consumption purposes.

In any event, the Arabs had considerable influence in southern Europe for many hundreds of years. Irrespective of the original source of distillation, during this period the skills were utilized and recorded often in the terms we still use today, for example the word for alcohol itself and the previously-mentioned alembic (pot still). It was during the 12th century that distillation began to be put into practice in Europe by people other than the Moors. It's likely that this happened in one of the labs associated with Europe's first higher-level medical school, in Salerno in what is now Italy.

Science was cultivated and disseminated not only in the educational institutions but also within the church via the monasteries. They studied the properties of alcohol and used it in solvents, medicines and essences. Alcohol's ability to dissolve both fats and water-soluble substances was an advantage. The fact that it made it possible to combine all manner of fragrant ingredients was probably also quite useful

for anyone who wanted to spice up the atmosphere within the monastery walls.

The knowledge spread both within and beyond Europe. There is evidence from both Italy and Spain, and even from China, that, from the 13th century onwards, wine was being used to produce liquor. It is interesting to note that the "water of life" was already being produced from grain in Ireland by the time commander Richard de Clare, also known as Strongbow, landed on the island with his Norman-English army in the 12th century. This can also be seen as the first justification for what became a reality a few hundred years later and remained so up until the 19th century, namely, that it was originally Ireland that was synonymous with whisky. If you consider all the historical facts, it becomes evident that the Irish were dominant in terms of the number of distilleries and quantities produced and also in terms of their reputation as whisky producers. Respect is certainly due to Scotland today, but for a long time the Scots remained at the stage of producing home-brew in their cottages while Ireland had developed licensed production, even if only using pot stills.

Looking at Europe more widely, the first evidence of liquor production in France dates from the 14th century. However, this French production got a big boost a couple of hundred years later, to such an extent that cognac came into being.

> "The Dutchman for a drunkard, the Dane for golden locks, the Irishman for whiskey, the Frenchman for the pox."
>
> John Marston, English playwright, 1604.
> Golden-haired Danes and Frenchmen with shameful afflictions – that's how it was in Shakespeare's time!

However, the birth of cognac was preceded by much earlier experiments aimed at discovering the fifth element. Professor of medicine Arnauld de Villeneuve attempted to unearth the mysteries of alchemy during the second half of the 13th century. The challenge was to find the fifth element, which, alongside the four others—earth, fire, water and air—was one of the constituent parts of matter. De Villeneuve believed he had found it and consequently it was named "quinta essentia", from which the word "quintessence" is derived. De Villeneuve was the first European to describe the process of alcohol distillation in detail.

When he familiarized himself with the results of the process, he believed he hadn't merely found the fifth element; he got so carried away that he deemed alcohol to be "the mother of all matter".

Because of the warming and beneficial effects alcohol had, he was quick to name this liquid "water of life", or, to use the phrase he himself is said to have used, eau de vie.

Local names for "water of life" have subsequently been determined by the local language. The effect appears to have been the same in view of what was, on the whole, a similar reaction to the warming drink resulting from distillation—from a wash of rice in China, and from wine in the Middle East and finally also in Europe. In terms of medicine, it was a good cure for all afflictions, from bad temper and ageing to gout, the plague and alcoholism. It was, quite simply, in the eyes of people at that time, life-giving. This was a perception that lasted for some time, and it is only relatively recently that the health implications of alcohol began to be discussed, including the notions of restraint and moderation.

Let us imagine, nevertheless, that Arnauld de Villeneuve fully lived up to the image of the genius familiar to us from Archimedes in his bath, the difference being that, as de Villeneuve threw his arms into the air, bursting with joy in the midst of his decoctions and minerals, his ears and nose were probably just a little red. And you already know what the water of life later came to be called in Gaelic: *Uisge beatha*, or *usquebaugh*, or in English, quite simply, whisky.

> "It prolongs life, removes ill temper, rejuvenates the heart and keeps one young."
>
> Arnauld de Villeneuve (1234–1311), on the "water of life."

Whisky in Scotland for the first time

Northern Britain was originally populated by the Picts. They got their name from the body paintings they adorned themselves with. Or was it because they carved pictures on rocks? Or because they had clothes with colored patterns? Take your pick. There are in fact today Pictish designs preserved on stones at some ancient sites and they reappear as reproductions, for example in several of the labels and symbols on various versions of Glenmorangie's whisky labeling and packaging.

The fate of the Picts has fallen into oblivion, since their disappearance from our history in about 900 AD is as poorly documented as their origins. However, during the great European migrations they were forced out by Celts who, arriving via what is now Ireland, populated what was to become Scotland from the beginning of the 5th century. The Celts brought to this part of north-western Europe their Gaelic language and their culture.

In 409 AD, the Romans left south-west Scotland. There, and in Ireland, the kingdom of Dál Riata was formed. St. Columba arrived in Scotland from Ireland in 563 and began to save Picts and Scots as fast as he could. It was in conjunction with this that Columba founded the monastery on the island of Iona, west of the Isle of Mull and about 12 miles west of Oban.

But now let's take a big leap forward into the Middle Ages. The first Scottish reference to proper whisky is normally considered to be an entry in the Exchequer Rolls (tax records) for 1494. The entry describes how the monk John Cor, from Lindores Abbey just north of the then Scottish capital Dunfermline, had bought in a considerable amount of malt, on the orders moreover of the whisky-loving King James IV of Scotland. In addition to his often-mentioned thirst, the king considered himself to be knowledgeable about medicine, and needed whisky to cure himself and others. Rather like you and your remedy for coughs and colds, I would imagine.

In the Exchequer Rolls it is apparent that John Cor's purchase consisted of "eight bolls of malt to Friar John

Cor, by order of the King, wherewith to make acqua vitae". That volume is the equivalent of about 2,600 pounds (1,200 kg) in weight. That's a lot of sacks of malt. Even if the yield was not as high as today's, it would still have been sufficient to make tens if not hundreds of gallons (or hundreds of liters) of whisky. Distillation was certainly an established practice by the time this entry was made, although it would have been mainly for medicinal purposes, and using wine as the raw material. What's amazing about the brief entry from 1494 is that, for the first time, it provides evidence of Scottish liquor distillation with barley as the raw material. Note also that it was in the Lowlands that it all started.

> "The Irish invented whisky, but only used it as a liniment for their sick mules. Only my fellow-countrymen would have thought of the idea of drinking whisky."
>
> Unknown Scottish poet.

Measurements of volume important to know

To make it clear how much barley malt John Cor bought, we can make a comparison with a legal letter dating from 1834. Admittedly this is a good three hundred years later, but roughly speaking the relationships between the units of measurement are the same as they relate to well-established goods and occupational sectors. The 19th century letter sets out the volumes of certain types of cereal and their corresponding weight. A bushel of barley is 54 pounds (24.5 kg) in weight.

A boll is equal to six bushels and John Cor bought "eight bolls of malt". If we assume that barley malt has a weight per volume similar to that of barley itself, some simple mathematical calculations tell us that John Cor had declared 54 x 6 x 8 which is equal to just under 2,600 pounds (1,200 kg) of malt. On the basis of a somewhat poorer yield than today, in terms of gallons of alcohol per pounds of malt, that would correspond to an expectation on the part of the monk of producing just over 100 gallons (around 300 liters) of whisky. Not a venture for an inexperienced amateur, in other words.

Bad beer and good liquor

The fact that distillates from grain emerged from Ireland and Scotland also has its explanation in practicalities. The availability of hops was limited due to the climate. Ale and other fermented beverages made from malt were not stable enough to be stored. Fermentation could not be controlled, as its secrets had not yet been revealed. The brew could turn out in one of several ways; it might be similar to the previous one if the woman of the house was clever enough to know that she needed to make use of earlier brews. Maybe there were strange tastes and smells from uncontrolled spontaneous fermentation, bubbling intriguingly due to yeast spores in the environment.

It's easy to understand the fascination with distillation at this stage. All of a sudden, a drink with a short shelf life became more long-lasting and acquired qualities that were far more intriguing than the mere fact that it could be kept for more than a week in the pantry and still be palatable. Also, if the harvest failed, a thrifty person could sell portions of the warming drink to bring money into the household. In addition, the ratio of volume to alcohol content decreased. That should have been good news for the tradesmen carrying gurgling casks through the mountains, or must at least have caused one or two mules to let out a loud hee-haw.

As in Sweden, flavors were added to the liquor to give it medical properties, and also to conceal imperfections in production, in other words fusel oil and off-flavors. It was not until the mid 18th century that people began to differentiate between flavored and unflavored whisky by designating the latter 'plain malt'. These days unflavored whisky is completely dominant. The nearest we come to flavored whisky today is the occasional special edition; for example, Compass Box spiced with orange peel, or cinnamon-packed Fireball, admittedly based on American whiskey.

Distilled wine and the beginning of maturation in casks

Wine had been traded in Europe since ancient times. One problem was that the wine didn't keep; on lengthy journeys it often turned sour. The Dutch came to the rescue when in the 16th century they learned how to distill wine to make *brandwijn*, or, in German, *Branntwein*, or *brandywine* in English—or simply brandy! In this instance, the purpose of distilling wine was to improve its shelf life and reduce its volume. There was also the idea that after it had been delivered it could be diluted with water to get back something that resembled the original wine. That was about as successful as trying to cycle backwards. However, the positive thing to come out of this flawed thinking was that people learned how to make brandy for the first time. Ta-da!

An important stage in the development of aromatic liquor came about thanks to a combination of Dutch brandywine and tragic religious persecutions in France. The years 1562 to 1598 comprised the period of the French Wars of Religion. The Catholics persecuted the Reformist Huguenots. Trade stagnated. Goods perished, became unusable or were sold off at a loss. The traders' distilled wine languished in casks in the warehouses while waiting to be shipped. That might seem like a bad situation but, as if through divine intervention, it was discovered that after the liquor had been stored, and once the tap was inserted into the cask, it was both smoother and fuller in flavor. This discovery laid the foundations of knowledge about the virtues of liquor maturation in casks.

Whisky—running like a thread through the history of Scotland

Initially mainly a feature of diet, the production of whisky became an issue for the legislature in 1579. It was decided at that point that the noble art of distilling malt liquor should be the preserve of the upper classes. The main reason for this was the

shortage of grain. This is the first significant historical reference to a link between whisky and politics. Interestingly, from this point onwards the history of whisky runs like a common thread through the history of Scotland. Perhaps we should see whisky as a sweetener in the otherwise bitter struggle between Scotland and England through the ages. Whisky was there in the background as clans and royalty, church and parliament plotted to gain power and argued with each other in the battle over unity and separation between the countries and their institutions.

It was following a decision in the Scottish parliament in 1644 that whisky was first taxed. Whisky was to act as a cash cow. What was milked from the cow went towards financing the fight against the rebels which was led, with some initial success, by the Marquis of Montrose in support of King Charles I. From the point of view of the whisky producers, the taxation decision caused barely a stir. Production

at this time was mainly small-scale and carried out clandestinely, and was therefore not affected by taxes. One larger-scale producer who was, however, hit doubly, or perhaps triply, was a family by the name of Forbes in Culloden. They were whisky producers and Protestants, and so opponents of the king who they were now to be financing through their taxes. The name of Forbes was to come up again in the debate about taxes a few decades later, once again on the occasion of civil unrest, as we shall soon see.

The first big distilleries

By the end of the 17th century, what was, for the time, large-scale production of whisky had been developed at a handful of distilleries. The most famous of these was Ferintosh in Ross, north of Inverness. The owner of Ferintosh was Duncan Forbes of Culloden. Forbes was not very popular amongst the Catholic Jacobites because of his support for the arch-Protestant William III of Orange. In the first place, William was Dutch. Secondly, he was a staunch Protestant, appointed during the revolution. Thirdly, as a result of his birth and deep-rooted habit, he had a fondness for Dutch gin. This was a cocktail of characteristics that didn't gain him any popularity in the Highlands. At this time, the British Isles too were suffering from the religious convulsions taking place in Europe. Following the Glorious Revolution in England in 1688, Protestants were chased up and down Scotland with halberds and pitchforks.

Union, rebellion and expansion

It was obvious that a successful Protestant like Duncan Forbes would become a victim of persecution. His distillery in Ferintosh was burned down in 1689, as were the Forbes family's other properties. In compensation, the now loyalist Scottish parliament exempted the Forbes family from taxation, and allowed whisky to be produced with a tax burden that was marginal in comparison to the general level at the time. The tax differential came to be even greater as time went on. The tax exemption had no time limit and covered whisky production provided it used barley from Forbes's own lands in Ferintosh and Bunchrew. Forbes's privilege survived the 1707 Act of Union but was abolished in 1785. In the rebellious atmosphere that prevailed in Scotland in the early 18th century, the Forbes family initially found it hard to take full advantage of the significant financial benefits parliament had bestowed upon them.

In pursuit of their claim to the throne, James Edward and his son Charles Edward Stewart of the Catholic Stewart family, made plans to revolt. Their plans came unstuck, however, and, in the case of the latter, spectacularly at Culloden in 1746. The English government troops finally crushed the rebellion with methods second only to Stalin's. The situation inside the country stabilized. The ensuing calm enabled Duncan's oldest son, John Forbes, to once again seek out customers all over Scotland, particularly in the larger towns—and you need to strike while the iron is hot. John Forbes exploited the family's tax exemption, buying more acreage for cereal-growing so that big bucks rolled in once Ferintosh began producing at maximum capacity. Business was excellent and Ferintosh sold so much that for a decade or so at the beginning of the 18th century the name Ferintosh became synonymous with whisky.

To the annoyance of those who had to pay tax and purchase a production license, the Forbes family produced what were considered large volumes at the time. They operated their business for about a hundred years, from the late 17th century onwards. During this period, the annual volume of whisky that was dispensed to the market increased steadily. In their last year of operation, the tax authorities noted that Ferintosh had produced no less than 100,000 gallons of raw whisky, equivalent to about 410,000 liters.

As Ferintosh was starting to gain momentum, a tax-paying whisky industry was also being built up alongside the Ferintosh distillery. A complicated set of rules and regulations and hefty tax rates made it a real challenge to produce whisky in accordance with legislation. In 1724, a malt tax was introduced in Scotland at the same level as in England to finance war against France. The malt tax forced the law-abiding producers to change their whisky for financial

reasons and use unmalted barley; the same happened in Ireland with both beer and whiskey. Even today, this is one of the things that distinguishes most Irish whiskey from Scottish whisky, and is also what distinguishes a medium-strong beer like Guinness from the often sweeter and stronger English stout.

Grain shortage and a ban on home-distilling

The grain shortage aggravated the situation further and also drove taxes up even higher. From 1757 to 1760, licensed whisky production was banned completely as a result of poor harvests. Note, however, that private production was still entirely permissible. In the face of this unsatisfactory state of affairs, the larger license-paying producers campaigned intensively for change. The Forbes family's tax exemption also irritated the hard-pressed license-paying producers.

Legal home-distilling wasn't popular either, and the problem was accentuated by its enormous scale. Around half of the whisky produced around 1780 came from home-distilling. Added to that, the home-distillers didn't make much effort to declare their product when it did go to the market. All in all, the tax-paying major producers felt they were being wronged, and that duties and regulations should naturally be relaxed and changed to their advantage.

The home-distillers, however, were delighted that the constant increases in tax rates provided a better pricing scenario for their own, often untaxed, product. The first hard-won victory for the tax-paying producers finally came in 1774. That year, the size of the still was regulated, and a minimum volume was set; this meant that distilleries had to have wash and liquor stills that held over 480 and 120 gallons respectively (about 1,800 and 450 liters respectively). That was a very high volume at the time, especially in view of the

fact that small stills were being used by the majority of producers. In 1779, home-distilling was restricted to stills holding a maximum of two gallons, about 9 liters, and then, in 1781, home-distilling was banned altogether. 1–0 to the major producers.

The Wash Act—Scotland is divided

The Forbes family's main competitors were the Haigs and the Steins. There was also a handful of other medium-sized distilleries besides their own. The Wash Act of 1784 divided Scotland up into the Highlands and the Lowlands. The dividing line— the Highland Line—was drawn between Greenock, west of Glasgow, and Dundee, south of Aberdeen. The aim of the new law was to provide an incentive for legal production, and it succeeded. In the north, tax rates were reduced for those who produced liquor from locally-grown barley. However, taxation continued to be based on the volume of the stills. In

the south, taxation was changed and was based on the volume of wash produced. For the Lowlands, the consequences were disastrous in the long run, since they led to a process whereby people maximized the amount of liquor they took from the wash instead of extracting the best of it. So, while it is true that the initiative succeeded in encouraging adherence to legal volumes in the Lowlands, success came at the price of quality. And, if truth be known, geographical distances, sparse population and inaccessibility meant that neither the government nor the Lowland Scots had much idea of what was actually going on, or what the effects of various decrees were, in the distant Highlands.

With the advent of the Wash Act, the Forbes family's tax exemption came to an end in 1785. Well-fed and prosperous having enjoyed the benefits of tax subsidy since 1689, the Forbeses were now shaken out of their comfortable existence, coming to the

ground with a resounding thud. Taxation had now caught up with them. To add to their worries, they didn't have in place the sort of well-honed business operation their competitors had been forced into by a hundred years of taxation. For the Forbeses, this resulted in financial crisis followed shortly by bankruptcy.

In Kilbagie, just over 10 miles northwest of Edinburgh where the Firth of Forth narrows, tax-paying major producer Robert Stein had established a distillery with an impressive daily output of no less than 6,000 gallons when fully operational, the equivalent of just over 22 cubic meters. The Haigs and the Steins were responsible at that time for no less than 50 percent of the whisky production in Scotland. Together with the other Scottish produc-ers, they flooded the English market with liquor, something that was viewed by the English producers with increasing concern. The Steins and the Haigs

were closely related—Robert Stein and John and James Haig were cousins—and in 1786 they shipped just over 1 million gallons (around 4 million liters) of liquor to England, which was mostly distilled again to be used as a base for gin production. To put these volumes into perspective, the Stein and Haig businesses were the biggest manufacturing enter-prises in the whole of industry to be in production during the first decade of Scottish industrialization from around 1779.

This massive influx into England led to a success-ful lobby that in 1788 pushed through tax rises and new regulations in respect of Scottish exports to England. For instance, it was demanded that the Scottish Lowland producers declare their upcoming sales volumes a year in advance. The consequence of this was that exports to England stopped for twelve months, with catastrophic results, as the fall in sales quickly drove several producers out of business. Five

also brought about the elimination of many smaller producers. When the Revolutionary Wars with France broke out in 1793, they were financed partly through a dramatic increase in whisky taxation from three to nine pounds per gallon of yearly distilling capacity. A bad situation therefore became worse, and even more producers had severe difficulties in keeping their businesses afloat.

A familiar pattern

The war against France brought about higher taxes. When creativity in terms of widening the tax base dried up, the government switched to increasing the tax levies already in existence. This affected whisky too. Following the pattern now familiar from history, illegal selling and smuggling increased. The Highland producers had also already been subjected to an export ban by the Wash Act less than a decade earlier. No doubt this was an irritation for the enlightened English and Southern Scots, many of whom felt Highland whisky was of the highest quality. The demand couldn't be satisfied through legal supply, and the consequence of this was extensive smuggling, which boomed in the decades around the turn of the 19th century. From the inaccessible valleys of Speyside and surrounding areas, the smugglers' routes went overland across the Grampians. Flavorsome Highland whisky found its clientele in the growing urban areas around Glasgow and Edinburgh and also in the more southerly parts of the kingdom. Smuggling was able to continue mainly because the estate owners—the lairds—turned a blind eye to what was going on. By horse-trading with the whisky producers, the lairds could themselves benefit from the producers' prosperity by making their property available to them so that both production and delivery of the goods could go ahead in peace and quiet.

of the larger distilleries, owned by the Steins and the Haigs, were forced to close down. The Steins' and Haigs' businesses also went bankrupt, with debts of £700,000 due to delays in receiving income. That's thought to be the equivalent of about £20 million in today's values, and was an enormous debt at the time. Production plummeted and from 1790 to 1794 there was no legal export of whisky to England at all. The Haigs and the Steins did however manage to return to the market after only a couple of years. This was made possible by financial backers who recognized that the problems were related to the attempts to take over the English market through price dumping. The families were therefore refinanced on the condition that they confined themselves to the Scottish market.

The change in the law which required advance notification of volume of production meant that the major producers had to sell the whisky intended for export in their domestic market at low prices. This

This operation became very widespread and well-organized. By the end of the 18th century, large

From bounty-hunters to orderly licensed production

There were a few clumsy attempts to change the rules around the turn of the 19th century, with the aim of tackling smuggling and illegal production. Successfully duping the taxman and producing illegal liquor had become a challenge for many people, as had the contest with the gaugers (or measurers). The battle between the illegal distillers and the gaugers often resulted in violence. In both camps, it was a question of survival. The gaugers' involvement was far from idealistic and could be explained more readily by the matter of their own financial gain. Earning only a minimal wage, the gaugers had to pay out of their own pockets for food, accommodation, wages and equipment for themselves and their colleagues. The only chance they had to make ends meet and make a few cents of profit was to keep the momentum going in the hunt for illegal liquor. They had the right to half the value of all the whisky they confiscated. The result was a taxman on commission who, using all possible means, became a bounty-hunter in a fierce battle against illegal distillers and smugglers.

One error on the way to reducing illegal distillation was the law of 1814 which banned stills holding less than 600 gallons, almost 2.3 cubic meters, in the Highlands. In practice, this was a ban on distilling, except in the case of a few large-scale producers. The smaller producers who chose to continue their business did so on the same scale as before, but became illegal overnight because their stills didn't meet the minimum volume requirement.

The consequences were obvious, which meant that by 1816 a more considered amendment to the law had been worked up. The Small Stills Act of that year abolished the distinction between the industries in the Highlands and the Lowlands. In addition, the Act legalized stills holding as little as 48 gallons, just under 200 liters, as well as a weaker wash. Allowing this size of still made it possible for smaller producers to operate legally but still required a relatively large

parts of Scotland derived their income from this illegal export industry which in time involved barley growers, coopers and coppersmiths. The smuggling routes went primarily from north to south. Amazing ingenuity went into keeping production hidden and getting goods out to the customers. There are many stories about how signaling systems were set up to warn that the taxman was on his way; for example, the officer might think he was being welcomed with flags when the signals were in fact to warn of his arrival. There are tales of tunnels used to divert smoke so that it wouldn't betray the distillation activity, and cunning hiding-places, such as whisky being stashed in both coffins and vestries.

volume, so that illegal distillers were prevented from using portable stills, which could be moved from pub to pub or into a new hiding-place when the gauger arrived. This encouraged the development of legal whisky production.

The result was plain to see—a three-fold increase in the number of legal distilleries, from 36 in 1816 to 125 three years later. The new law also meant that the lairds started to change their views on illegal whisky. Smuggling and illegal distilling often brought violence and other criminal activity in their wake. The result was that the landowners themselves established distilleries, in some cases leading to skirmishes between the lairds and the illegal distillers. However, the legal system was still lagging behind in the fight against illegal distillers. They were to maintain their grip on the market for a few more years, before new changes in the law made legal production an even more attractive option.

The basis of the industry of today—the Excise Act

Let's illustrate the extent of illegal distilling and smuggling in a few more figures before we have a look at the Act itself. At the time of the Excise Act of 1823 and the decision to revise legislation relating to whisky production, the legal volume of production was around 3½ million gallons per year, the equivalent of just under 14 million liters. Five years later, the volume of legally-produced whisky had risen to 12 million gallons, 46 million liters, per year. The difference can largely be explained by a movement from illegal distilling to licensed production. Since 90% of the whisky was sold within Scotland, it can be assumed that demand during this relatively short period remained fairly constant. To add to these figures on volume, there's the somewhat sensational figure of 14,000 illegal stills seized in 1823—almost 300 per week!

they were aware of the activity or not. The Act was followed a year later with a new tax law relating to whisky production, the Excise Act.

The Excise Act of 1823 brought about a halving of the tax rate and also introduced an annual fee of £10 for a production license. Other provisions in the Act included tax-free warehousing and free export. All in all, this was an enormous improvement in conditions for tax-paying producers. Producers were immediately afforded a good deal of freedom in how they set up their production, in terms of both wort strength and mash bills and also the size and shape of the still. Within about ten years, the number of distilleries had multiplied, and the illegal trade had made an unexpectedly swift exit.

As an aside, it should nevertheless be noted that the political debate on alcohol in Scotland had not yet addressed the issue of temperance. As yet, whisky was mainly the subject of discussions only when the topic was tax revenue, illegal distilling and smuggling. This was, however, to change within a couple of decades owing to a growing temperance movement.

The first person to get a license for legal production in accordance with the new law was Captain George Smith. With financial assistance from the estate

It's hard to believe that you could open a cupboard door in Scotland at that time without a swan-necked copper still falling out. And surely no-one imagined that the stills that were collected in were all that existed! A figure for comparison: in 1832, the number of court cases for illegal distilling had fallen to a modest 85. Legal production had won.

The start of this transformation was the speech made in parliament in 1820 by one of the most important estate owners, the Duke of Richmond and Gordon. His position was that legal production should be made easier and that the authorities should crack down harder on illegal production. In his opinion the measures included in the legislation between 1816 and 1818 should be extended. He got the support of parliament, and the result was the Illicit Distillation Act of 1822 with steeply increased penalties for illegal distillation and smuggling. One implication of the new law was that estate owners could be prosecuted for unlawful distilling on their property, whether

> "… an extraordinary change was soon perceived; smuggling was greatly suppressed, and for one gallon that was permitted in the country from my distillery previous to 1823, there were, from that time till 1830, an increase of from thirty to forty times."
>
> Captain Munro, Teaninich Distillery, looking back in 1835, and seeming to be in no doubt that the legislation had been beneficial.

owner the Duke of Gordon, he founded his Glenlivet distillery in Upper Drumin in the area of Minmore, a little higher up the hillside than it is today, in 1824. Smith's business concept was to sell high-quality malt whisky to the rapidly growing industrial areas in the Lowlands. Smith became a direct threat to the illegal distillers. In their eyes he was a strikebreaker, and he was therefore subjected to death threats and also to threats to burn down his distillery. Smith was given a pair of pistols by his financial backers so that he could defend himself. The Smith family owned the Glenlivet distillery right up to 1978 when it was bought by Seagram's, at the same time as the Glen Grant distillery was acquired.

By the end of 1825, the 111 licensed distilleries of 1823 had more than doubled in number to 263. The legislators took that as confirmation that their aims had been achieved. Almost two hundred years later, what is clear to us is that the new law formed the basis of the modern whisky industry. Legal whisky production was also driven by the fact that the change in law came at the right time. The market got closer to the producers through improved communications, and new technical solutions arose as a result of the increasingly insistent rumbling progress of industrialization.

"The king o' drinks, as I conceive it, Talisker, Isla, or Glenlivet!"

Robert Louis Stevenson

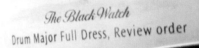

The Black Watch
Drum Major Full Dress, Review order

The Highlanders
Pipe Major No.1 Dress, Playing in Mess

SINGLE MALT   ELGIN   SCOTCH WHISKY   CLASSIC

GLEN MORAY

SPEYSIDE SINGLE MALT SCOTCH WHISKY

AGED **16** YEARS

Finest Quality since 1897

Drummer 1787   Captain 1900   Private 1909   Sergeant 1790

The Argyll &
Sutherland Highlanders

...D AND BOTTLED IN SCOTLAND BY THE GLEN MORAY...

The clan culture that came in from the cold

After the battle of Culloden, anything to do with the culture of the clans was prohibited in British public life. So, it was a major vindication when George IV visited Edinburgh in 1822, the first English monarch to do so since 1633. Until this event, the culture, clothing and music of the clans had been viewed with disdain in England and also in Lowland Scotland. Things were now changing in Scotland, whose densely-populated southern parts were fumbling for a national identity and whose northern part had been treated like the poor relation for several decades. The royal visit in 1822 gave Scottish nationalism a real boost. The visit was in addition stage-managed by the very popular Scottish Romantic Sir Walter Scott. The welcome drink? Whisky of course. And dress? Tartan-patterned, naturally. Even the king was dressed up as a clan chieftain—although he was said to have had long pink underpants on underneath. The lengths a prudish monarch will go to to hide the Crown Jewels!

The royal visit and the blessing of the whisky had far-reaching consequences. They contributed hugely both to the work of introducing whisky into social circles and at the same time to making it politically acceptable as an important product for Great Britain as a whole.

The demand for whisky took another leap forward when Queen Victoria began to spend time at Balmoral Castle, going on grouse-shooting expeditions and reading Sir Walter Scott. What could then be more natural than to publicly divulge a liking for whisky? In truth, these Scottish-related events drove sales of whisky more than the fact that the queen actually also visited Ireland in 1849. Gradually, snifter-drinking English gentlemen were persuaded that their brandy could be replaced by a good whisky. The queen's soft spot for the Highlands also rubbed off, positively, on Ireland.

> "... pure Glenlivet whisky; the king drank nothing else."
>
> Elizabeth Grant of Rothiemurchus
> (1797–1886, "The Highland Lady",
> authoress and social commentator)

The number of Scottish distilleries from 1823 to today

The number of distilleries currently operating—just over one hundred—is low in historical terms. This can largely be explained by the fact that productivity today is greater than in the past. The fact that numbers have fallen drastically, especially from 1823 onwards, is also because the distilleries in existence when the 1823 law was enacted were in many cases small in comparison with those which have since come into being. Here are some additional comments relating to the shape of the curve:

» Decrease in 1860 due to tax rises in the Spirits Act of that year.

» Increase from this date until the 1890s, thanks to the sales upturn brought about by blended whisky.

» Decrease again after 1900 until the First World War, due firstly to over-production in the late 1890s, then the Pattison Crash and a few years later the consequences of the war.

» In 1920, there's a brief recovery after the war before prohibition and the Great Depression intervene. Note that the industry twitched briefly into life again after prohibition but that it then declines until the end of the Second World War. (The number of active distilleries fluctuates considerably from year to year, but this is not always reflected in the graph.)

» Upswing until the oil crisis, then another positive trend reversal around the 1990s.

Finally, it's worth noting that the diagram shows the number of distilleries and not volume. This is amply demonstrated in that, in 1910, 124 distilleries produced only 29% more whisky by volume than a mere 64 distilleries supplied by volume in 1935.

(Source of statistics: The Whiskies of Scotland by R. J. S. McDowall and The Making of Scottish Whisky by Michael S. Moss and John R. Hume.)

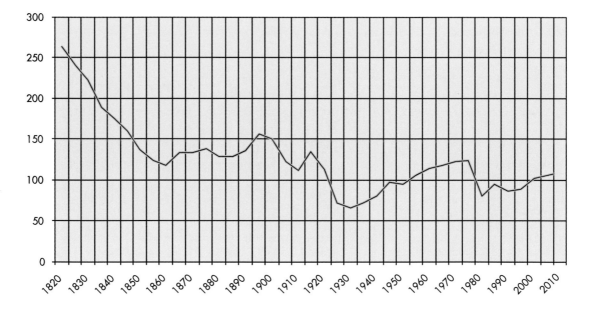

Whisky's triumph, and the question: "What is whisky?"

The distilling industry prospered from the beginning of the 1820s. There was a market initially in the remarkably fast-expanding urban areas of Edinburgh and Glasgow, but also further south and soon enough also in other parts of the Empire. Demand increased, and a process was needed that was more effective than the long-winded and slow batch distillation in pot stills. The first step towards a more rational process was taken by the major producer Robert Stein, who ran a number of distilleries in the Lowlands. In 1826 he invented a basic column still which enabled liquor to be distilled more quickly from grain using a more continuous method.

The next step in development was taken by a former Inspector General of Excise, the Irishman Aeneas Coffey. In 1830, Coffey patented his improved column still. Roughly speaking, the principles are the same even today, although there have been considerable improvements in the last two hundred years. Coffey's continuous still went into production for the first time in 1834 at John Philp & Co. Coffey's fellow Irishmen sneered at the newfangled equipment, saying that real whiskey could only be made in a pot still. This negative view of developments and the haughty pronouncements would soon enough give people in the Irish whiskey industry reason to keep quiet. It was an attitude that would be questioned by future generations of Irish whiskey producers. Unfortunately, the industry heirs would not have the option of reconsidering and rectifying their strategy when faced with the fait accompli left by their predecessors.

The column still was, however, quickly adopted in Scotland. The years that followed were a triumphal march for grain whisky, partly because of the increased efficiency and partly because of the smooth characteristics of the liquor that the technique

produced. Thirteen column distilleries were started in the Lowlands within fifteen years. The Scots saw their opportunity to increase both volumes and margins. This enabled them to curtail the still dominant Irish, who turned up their noses at continuous distillation using both corn and other grain as the base.

Grain whisky was purer and therefore milder in taste, which made it more commercially attractive. It was more accessible in terms of both taste and also volume than the more demanding, more flavorsome, batch-produced malt whisky. Through these fundamental advantages, grain whisky and the column still technique were to revolutionize drinking habits in much of the world during the next 50 years.

The new technique also gave momentum to the dispute about what was real whisky. On the one side were the traditionalists, such as the Irish, who clung to their pot stills. The Highland Scots were also rooting for them, as they could see the danger of being driven out of business by grain whisky. The English, accustomed to brandy, happily drank the milder grain whisky from the Lowlands. On the other side were those producers who were pro-development and perhaps more market-sensitive, who realized that the mild and clean grain whisky had a bigger market; its lighter and dryer tone meant that it could appeal to a wider public who were not simply after a potent, oily whisky for their hip-flask during the grouse-shoot.

An ingenious combination

An important step forward for the promotion of whisky and reduction of production costs came when Andrew Usher & Co. began to sell a blended whisky. There are records stating that this product, "Old vatted Glenlivet whisky", was sold in London as early as 1844, but more consistent information suggests 1853, with export sales from 1864. To start with, admittedly, this was just a mixture of Glenlivet whisky and other malt whiskies, in other words a blended malt. Within a few years a blend conforming to modern descriptions would come into being, i.e. a mixture of both malt and grain whisky. This was sold under the name Green Stripe, and is often cited as the world's first blended whisky. The idea of blending

came mainly from France. The lack of brandy following the ravages of the phylloxera vine aphid had enforced a leveling in quality between the old and the new from the storage cellars. A more domestic version of the background has Usher's wife, Margaret Balmer, as the creative force behind the idea; she was apparently a good blender of drinks.

Then, as now, the blend was a mixture of grain and malt whisky. And then, as now, it was a stroke of genius in at least four ways: it reduced costs by using grain whisky; it softened the character of the drink by combining neutral whisky with a flavorsome variety; it enabled producers to create their own taste and aroma profile by selecting their own blend of types of malt whisky; and, it made it possible to maintain a continuous profile, since it is the aroma and the taste which are the essential elements and not the ingredients.

A colored postcard view of Bowmore

Usher continued to blend, and was soon followed by a couple of colleagues in the industry. The technique was refined. By chance, in an event that proved lucky for the Scots but unlucky for vines, much of the European wine-making industry was laid waste, starting with the Rhône Valley in 1863. Grapevines had arrived from the US accompanied by the vine aphid *Phylloxera vastatrix*, now known as *Daktulosphaira vitifoliae*. The aphid attacks both the leaves and the roots of the vines and destroys them. The American vines had evolved a resistance to the aphids which the European vines did not have. Due to lax quarantine regulations, the aphids spread on an epidemic scale, and hit the European wine industry very badly. Despite emerging events, 1875 was a very good year for the wine producers. Due to the aphids, however, it was not surpassed until 1893. In the period between 1879 and 1886, the red wine market was in ruins.

In 1872, the aphid hit Charente, where cognac is produced. The attack was to transform the entire liquor industry and also the drinking habits of the world. By the 1880s, the aphid, with the kind assistance of blended whisky, had brushed brandy aside. The lack of an alternative in particular meant that whisky became acceptable even in respectable circles. Between 1880 and the turn of the century, production of cognac fell by two thirds. Any money raised by the small-scale producers, who in some cases were forced to sell their stills, was put towards acquiring aphid-resistant vines.

Until this disaster affected the wine industry, whisky had been seen more as just a warmer during the grouse-shoot than as something to accompany the coffee; more sport than port, perhaps? Now, however, with a crying need and few alternatives, whisky was good enough. At first the softer Irish whiskeys made

W & J. MUTTER'S

"They gave evidence that there was increased demand for whiskey of a milder kind, and that blends of pot still and patent still whiskey were in large demand by the consumers ..."

Observation from a special parliamentary committee in 1891 (the Select Committee of the House of Commons).

BOWMORE ISLAY.

WHISKY

it into the parlor, then the Scottish whisky. The often rougher Scottish whiskies were softened up by blending. That in itself helped to make whisky's character resemble brandy's more closely. With maturation increased from one or two years to several, whisky once again became more presentable. It appealed to discerning palates in England, where they were accustomed to smooth brandy. Blending with grain whisky and a longer maturation process would also prove to be a magic formula for acquiring customers beyond the British Isles too.

In the latter part of the 19th century, Scottish and Irish malt liquor was exported throughout the world with great success. At this stage, the Irish whiskey with its smooth, rich, pot still character had long had a substantial advantage, but the Scots were about to take the initiative. The Irish advantage lay in the fact that whiskey from the Emerald Isle was more

to people's tastes, and also because historically Irish production capacity was much greater. At the end of the 1850s, demand for Irish whiskey was around five times greater in volume than for Scottish whisky, and moreover demand was increasing, according to The Distillers Company themselves. But the trends were to change. The Scots were to take over the technical developments, and would in so doing improve the financial viability of production and also have greater success in global marketing. The biggest mistake made by the Irish, stubborn as mules, was to refuse to adopt the column still and, with that, the idea of blended whiskey.

This stance soon resulted in a declining share of the market. Cheaper blended whisky and also grain whisky from Scotland took the market by storm. As noted previously, this new Scottish whisky had a milder taste than the raw Scottish malt whisky. Like

the Irish whiskey, the new Scottish version was easier to embrace by those whose palates were used to soft grape distillates and who were looking for alternatives to the cognac which had dried up because of the ravages of the vine aphids on the other side of the Channel.

Upward trend with a blip

Whisky has maintained its strong position since the aphid attack. It's worth noting that the French these days drink a good deal more whisky than brandy. As industrialization and the opportunities that came with it unfolded, so whisky also developed as a product. The development of bottling, blending and labeling were important for taste profiling, packaging and marketing. In retrospect, it's possible to single out five companies who persuaded the English, then accustomed to cognac, to switch from mild Lowlands whisky to the newly-fashionable blended whisky. They captured London, England, and the scene was then set for a magnificent performance in the rest of the world. The five were John Dewar, James Buchanan with his Black & White brand, James L. Mackie with White Horse, John Walker, and lastly John Haig.

> *"The Irish sort is particularly distinguished for its pleasant and mild flavour. The Highland sort is somewhat hotter..."*
>
> Samuel Johnson, writer and lexicographer, who described this difference between whisky and whiskey in his Dictionary of the English Language as early as 1755. Johnson was also the first person to formulate the word "whisky" in the written form familiar today.

One or two of these, like the Chivas Brothers with Chivas Regal, Berry Brothers & Rudd with Cutty Sark, Matthew Gloag & Sons with Famous Grouse, and a few others, were expansionary wine merchants and whisky-selling general dealers who had been selling carpets, tea, wine and whisky from the beginning or middle of the 19th century. Through hard work and skillful exploitation of the marketing and distribution opportunities of the time, they grew at an impressive rate.

Walkers of Kilmarnock started their shop in 1820 and their angled label was established as early as 1867. Tommy Dewar dashed around the world at tireless speed to be ready to offer the company's whisky to royalty or other potentates during state visits, dinners or other similar events. Dewar got a cask into the White House via the steel magnate Andrew Carnegie; highly appropriate for the company which, in 1863, launched "White Label" as the world's first bottled whisky with a paper label, a world record they fight over with both Andrew Usher and the Mackinlay family. Great Britain's presence in all parts of the world also had considerable influence due to its established infrastructure. Within the Empire's internal markets, shipments were also made easier by low customs duties.

A curiosity in the history of whisky brand names is the court decision of 1880 that the name Glenlivet could only be used as an addition to the name of the distillery, except in the case of the original, Glenlivet in Drumin in Speyside. Following the court ruling, the place name had to come first, e.g. "Tomintoul-Glenlivet", for all but the original. The root of the judgment was in the fact that other producers had started to take advantage of Glenlivet's good name in bold type. Glenlivet had a good reputation and, by this time, a tradition going back fifty years of high-quality whisky production. Somewhat mockingly, the glen of the River Livet was called the longest glen in Scotland. It had more distilleries and was more extensive than even the most charitable cartographer could have conjured up.

In 1877 the column still distilleries in Scotland joined forces to form The Distillers Company (DCL). Together they were to engage in a battle with all those who were using print and pressure of all kinds to try to prevent grain whisky from qualifying as real whisky.

A pamphlet was published, with the willing support of Irish distilleries, with hard-hitting wording about insipid, neutral, grain liquor. The pamphlet stated that the writers were fighting "to control the fraudulent businessmen who were selling "silent spirit", disguised and flavored in various ways, but nevertheless named whisky". The contest was decided after a number of rounds, the first in 1891. That year, after cross-examining a number of experts, a specially-appointed parliamentary committee reached the conclusion that the addition of liquor from column stills was not adulteration but was simply diluting the drink, that it should therefore be considered legal, and that the blend could be called whisky. However, the battle continued in 1905 when people in a part

of London, in the Borough of Islington, went to the police to ask what constituted whisky. The provocative question was aimed mainly at local pub-owners. Increasingly, what they sold was not considered by the consumers to be the genuine article; it could be brandy mixed with grain liquor, pure and unmatured grain liquor and heavily-diluted malt whisky. Incidentally, it is true that at this time whisky was seldom matured for more than the odd year; in other words, it went direct from the still to the mouth.

"The Irish invented whisky, it was perfected by us."

Another unknown Scottish thinker, full of nationalism, modesty, and perhaps also whisky…

DCL pressed on with their action to save the reputation of grain whisky. After a long drawn-out process and pressure from both Islington's council officers and DCL, the chairman of the Chamber of Commerce agreed that a royal commission should be set up to look at the issue.

A large number of witnesses, industry experts, chemists and others were cross-examined between 1908 and 1909. Attempts were made to agree more culturally-determined definitions as well as exact chemical formulas. Thankfully, none of these were successful. Finally in 1909 it was confirmed in law that liquor produced in column stills, even if made from raw materials other than barley malt, could be called whisky. This was later supplemented by a legal provision in 1915 that stipulated that whisky should be matured for over two years; in 1916 this was changed to three years, to enable raw liquor also to be called

TIME MARCHES ON!

It makes me proud to think I've seen
The paddle-boat become the "Queen."
Like Clyde-built ships, I've grown in fame –
The skill behind me's still the same.

JOHNNIE
WALKER
SCOTCH WHISKY
Born 1820 –
still going
strong

whisky. This was a decision made with the demons of World War I in the background, and was subsequently viewed as a sure way to get stores to last at least three more years.

People who believed that only pot stills and barley could make a product worthy of the name whisky now took up arms in the struggle to define whisky. However, the debate collapsed like a failed soufflé following statements made by, of all people, the malt whisky devotees. The renegades were representatives from malt whisky distilleries, including the respected Long John MacDonald from Ben Nevis and Alexander Walker of Cardhu. They put forward their view that grain whisky could of course be called whisky, provided it didn't comprise more than half of the mixture. What brought about this turnaround is up for discussion, but they probably realized that their chances of surviving as malt whisky producers

depended then as now on finding a market for their malt whisky through a blender with a high volume of sales. John MacDonald summarized it all for the royal commission with the following well-judged words: "If it were not for the Highland malt, Scotch whisky would be practically non-existent and but for the toning-down by Lowland grain whisky, it would not have obtained its worldwide popularity." The detail in the legislation of 1909/1915 enabled the concept of whisky (actually spelled 'whiskey' at that time!) to be clarified. Moreover, it happened in such a way that it opened up opportunities for the industry to efficiently manufacture a great product for an ever-expanding market throughout the world.

In 1898, there was a real setback for the whisky industry and the rise of the whisky barons. After a couple of decades of expansion and an increasingly stretched industry literally deluging the Empire with

whisky, the events that were to come were absolutely in keeping with tulip bulbs and other bubbles. The Klondyke atmosphere in the industry evaporated as did the castle in the air built up by Pattison, Elder & Co in Leith. The company was run from Leith by brothers Robert and Walter Pattison, and their business partner Alexander Elder looked after the office in London. At that time, Pattison's was one of the largest blenders in existence. They became known for their extravagant ways and their carpet-bombing approach to marketing. This included teaching parrots to squawk the company's name and placing them in a number of well-chosen pubs in London.

The Pattison brothers became known on the whole for greatly prioritizing quantity and sales income over quality. Because of the sales they had built up, they became important customers at many of Scotland's distilleries. They had also tied the producers into

agreements to keep a certain volume in store for future sales. The crash happened because irregularities were discovered in the way the Pattisons managed both their finances and their operations. By 1894, the Board of DCL had already noted that the Pattisons' finances were "very doubtful".

The Pattison brothers persisted with their way of working, including tampering with the whisky. Typically for the circumstances, the Pattisons ventured into a tangle of substantial loans and oversubscribed share issues with fancifully-inflated valuations and suspect security. When the facade *did* finally begin to crumble,

◀ *William Grant (1839–1923), founder of Glenfiddich and Balvenie.*

it took only a few months for the whole business to collapse like a pile of leaky oak casks. The ringleaders themselves rightly ended up in prison. The tragic aspect of the whole carousel was that nine suppliers went bust. Dewar's and William Grant were two of the many companies who suffered greatly from the crash. There were large sums of money in circulation: at the time the Pattisons had debts of £300,000, an amount around 35 times greater at today's values or about £12 million.

◄ *Charles Gordon married into the Grant family in 1897 and then traveled around the world selling Glenfiddich. This is one of his well-filled address books.*

Short Sunderland flying boat on Loch Indaal during the Second World W...

War, prohibition, and other misery

Around the time of the First World War, there was a debate in Britain, as there was in many other countries, around liquor prohibition and alcohol damage. It came as a natural progression of the concern caused by unemployment, reduced pay and alcohol abuse almost a century earlier. The temperance movement in Scotland actually started in October 1829, during the depression of that time. The first Temperance Society was formed in Greenock, west of Glasgow, and other societies spread like wildfire across the whole country in a short space of time.

> *"...drink is doing us more damage in the war than all the German submarines put together."*
>
> David Lloyd George

At the time of the First World War, David Lloyd George, a teetotaler and later Prime Minister, held an animated debate on restricting production and consumption of alcohol. Amongst his opponents was a well-known whisky-lover, namely Winston Churchill. Lloyd George was keen to present Russia and France as good examples, as they had introduced restrictions on vodka and absinthe respectively.

A well-known comment from Lloyd George which had a bearing on this, and also alluded to the fact that alcohol production consumed enormous amounts of edible cereal, was that *"...drink is doing us more damage in the war than all the German submarines put together."* Lloyd George, who was Minister of Munitions until he became Prime Minister in 1916, wanted to remedy both the food shortage and alcoholism by doubling the tax on alcohol. He didn't succeed with this until 1917, but a range of other measures in the same vein were pushed through before that.

Ironically, one or two of the measures designed to reduce consumption seemed to be extremely positive for the long-term survival of whisky. The intelligent and commonsense approach that was taken, despite a teetotal Prime Minister inclined to prohibition, is often credited to an experienced administrator at the Department of Munitions. He is said to have gracefully steered the Prime Minister in a sensible direction. The administrator was James Stevenson, known to be both ambitious and conscientious, who had worked for both Lloyd George and, later, Winston Churchill. Stevenson's diligence led to his far too premature death, in 1926, at the age of 53, exhausted by both the war and by mammoth projects such as the construction of the old Wembley Stadium combined with responsibility for the British Empire Exhibition in 1924–25. Stevenson's passion for the "water of life" came about naturally, however. Before the war he was the managing director of John Walker & Sons, responsible amongst other things for coming up with the Striding Man, a distinguishing feature for Johnnie Walker even today.

Stevenson's contribution to the legislation included the reduction in the regulated alcohol content for domestic sales from 43% to 40%, as well as the introduction of the requirement that whisky should be matured for at least three years, starting from 1916. This made prices rocket by the equivalent of 20 pence per bottle to 63 pence overnight. The good thing to emerge from a bad situation was that stocks were made to last a little longer, in a situation where all the alcohol from column distilleries was being used by the war effort and where malt whisky production had been forced to shut down in 1917 so that there would be enough grain for food needs. The ban lasted until 1919 and was also combined with an export ban in 1918. The effects of this lasted well into the 1920s, intensified by the recession at the beginning of that decade. On top of that, alcohol prohibition in the US added considerably to the load. Against all the odds, however, the US ban did not cause as big a decline as expected for the Scots. Alcohol prohibition—the

Volstead Act—was brought in in the US in 1920. The Scots, in despair but maintaining their composure, handled it better by increasing production for storage. A certain volume was exported legally to the Bahamas and other intermediate destinations. From there, the whisky could be illegally transported into the US by Capone, Captain Bill McCoy and others.

In the case of Ireland, prohibition in the US wrecked whiskey sales to such an extent that they have not recovered even today. The Irish sat and witnessed it all from the western side of the Irish Sea. Their reaction was more one of paralyzed dismay, and also naive submissiveness to the ban. The Irish sat by and watched while one of their best markets was destroyed.

When prohibition came to an end in 1933, the Scots were able to start exporting again from their stores. During the period, the Irish had won the battle to become an independent republic in 1921 through civil war and conflicts with Britain. To add to the

strain, liberation had resulted in a number of pressures including a trade embargo from 1916 onwards. This seriously shrank the export market that the Empire had provided full access to before 1921. The conflicts with England also meant that whiskey exports to the rest of Britain declined drastically. The Irish whiskey industry was, to put it mildly, somewhat impaired by the time the ban was lifted in the US. There was no energy to meet the demand that suddenly once again surged from the west from 1933.

The Irish whiskey industry's self-importance and resistance to development at the end of the 19th century had taken its toll. One contributory factor in Ireland's fall from dominance that is often mentioned is mudslinging from illegal distillers in the US. Irish whiskey was the best seller in the US before 1920, and so it would have been natural to exploit its good reputation. If there is any truth at all in the allegation

that American illegal distillers called their rat poison Irish Whiskey, it can hardly have increased the popularity of the genuine product.

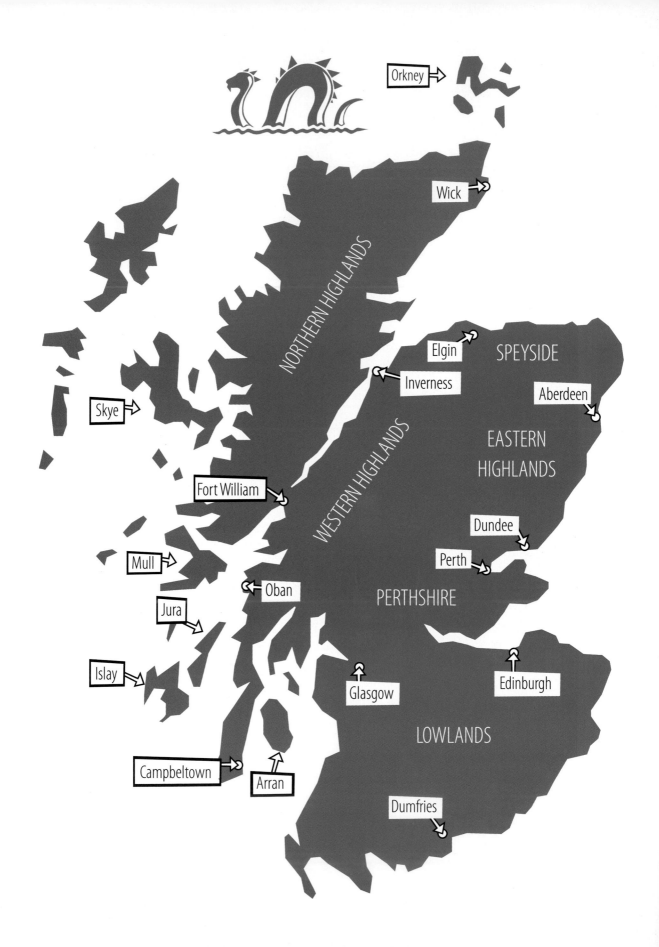

THE DISTRICTS

In the good old days—in a modern whisky context that's about twenty years ago—whisky was rightly divided into a handful of regions on the basis of taste and aroma. Maybe you laid the foundations of your interest in whisky by starting with the Six Classic Malts? If so, you'll be familiar with a Scotland divided into six regions in which parts of the country such as Glenkinchie, Oban and Lagavulin are represented. These areas are largely a commercial construct, an idea from Diageo's marketing department if you like. However, it's been a successful idea which has clearly helped to stimulate interest in whisky. The division into areas helped to categorize whisky, providing a potential tool, now much-utilized, for comparing regions, types and tastes. The origin of this segmentation, apart from Scottish geography itself, is, to a degree, the 1784 tax legislation that divided Scotland down the middle. With the divide as a starting point, the legislation governed the way whisky stills and production should work. These legal districts have been expanded, and the current division can be seen both as pandering to the public and as a sales tool. The division is a brilliant innovation, which makes explicit the unifying similarities between producers in various parts of Scotland. Today, however, the regional differences have become more and more blurred. It is of course entirely possible to produce both a smoky whisky in the middle of Speyside and an Irish-inspired triple-distilled whisky in Campbeltown, and, what's more, that is exactly what's happening!

The Lowlands

If you are a whisky traveler coming from the south, you might pass York, leave England and not notice much of a change in the landscape. You'll still see undulating hills, wooded areas, villages and towns passing at frequent intervals. In the far south of Scotland, there's an area known in whisky circles and often in other contexts as the Lowlands. The area consists of several counties and the northerly border is usually drawn as a line between Dundee and Greenock, outside Glasgow. Historically, large volumes, often triple-distilled, have been produced in large stills for export to England and other places to be used as the raw material for gin and other drinks.

The fact that the liquor has been sold in large quantities as semi-manufactured goods, with customers requiring a high level of purity, has meant that the whisky has become light and in many people's opinion much too lacking in character. In the modern age, when fashionable taste demands complexity and extravagant aromas, Lowlands whisky has come off increasingly badly. The approach has backfired to such an extent that there are now only a few distilleries left in this large and densely-populated part of Scotland. A few of the producers you'll recognize that are still active are Auchentoshan, Bladnoch, and Glenkinchie. Maybe you have also on some happy occasion sampled whisky from either the Rosebank or St Magdalene distillery, both disused but memorable? If you haven't, be sure to permit yourself that pleasure. It's light whisky, for sure, but there is character there, especially in its older years. It has freshness, citrus tones and a mild house character, bearing out the ability of their skillful producers to source good oak casks and make full use of them.

Highlands, Perthshire

In the middle of Scotland, in the Southern Highlands, we find the county of Perthshire, which is sometimes mentioned by name in the context of whisky. There are a number of distilleries here, including Aberfeldy, Deanston, Glenturret, and Blair Athol with their neighbor Edradour, and also Tullibardine. The whisky from this area can perhaps be said to have a common denominator consisting of a smooth, malty richness and mild smoky tones. In my opinion, this is an excellent whisky to enjoy on a Sunday afternoon with a good book.

Highlands, Speyside

Perhaps the most famous part of Scotland, Speyside is also the area with most distilleries. Its name comes from the River Spey that rises in the Grampian Mountains. They tower over the moors and run in an east–west direction just over an hour's drive north of Edinburgh. Previously an obstacle preventing the taxman from finding the illegal distillers on the northern side of the mountains, the Grampians now present a slow uphill climb for us tight-fisted tourists with a hired

Vauxhall too feeble for the trip to Speyside. The Speyside of today is a whisky paradise for those who love Scotland, always fighting for the whisky tourists with the island of Islay. In Speyside there are celebrity whiskies such as nutty, orange-toned The Macallan, the malty Cragganmore, sherry-influenced Glenfarclas, fresh Glenfiddich with notes of pear, and many many more. With just under fifty distilleries in the area, it's difficult to characterize the whiskies, even taking account of history. However, the classic Speyside character could perhaps be described as very mildly peaty, with a rich malty body topped with aromas of apple and pear and with a touch of slightly jammy, sherry tones.

Northern Highlands

Further north we arrive at a landscape which no longer has trees but has goodness knows how many fluffy sheep sauntering along roads and heather-clad moorland. The landscape is more barren here, the coastlines steeper and the need for whisky seems ever more obvious. Well-known producers in the northernmost part of Scotland include Balblair, Clynelish, Dalmore, Glenmorangie, and Old Pulteney. What was a rich characteristic in the Southern Highlands becomes even richer here; the sweetness of malt is fine-tuned with more of the heather honey and if you're very lucky there'll be a spicy peaty tone to tighten it all up. Need I mention that there are disused distilleries whose whisky you can try? You don't want to leave this earth without trying an old Brora, believe me.

Islands

For historical reasons, the peripheral parts of Scotland often have a peatier character. Peat has been the best fuel available to people out in the countryside and on the islands; thank goodness for that, because in general producers here have held onto a traditional aroma and taste profile which has elements of peat smoke. As a visitor to the islands, you'll be met by vertical cliffs, foaming waves and hospitable people. However, you'll probably only see the latter as everything else will be covered in low cloud and mist. The whisky from the islands ranges from the generously fruity Highland Park to the peppery Talisker and the slightly oily, salty Tobermory. Typical for most, however, is a more or less distinct peaty smokiness.

Islay

As one of the islands in what's called the Inner Hebrides, this island is something special in the world of whisky. The explanation lies in the numbers; there are just over 3,000 inhabitants with eight distilleries. Even the tax authorities scarcely know how much is actually produced—surely it's not just the wool that's keeping the very welcoming and friendly islanders warm? With all its distilleries and different types of whisky, Islay currently doesn't exactly have a clearly-defined style either. Just compare a Bruichladdich matured in a wine barrel with an unfiltered ten-year-old Laphroaig. Otherwise, for most people, Islay says smokiness, saltiness, phenols and sea; flavored with sherry casks or just with elements of a house character with diesel-like oiliness or malty sweetness.

Campbeltown

Farthest to the south west, in the direction of Ireland, lies the Kintyre peninsula. Halfway down the western side of the peninsula, ferries leave for Islay. If you continue on winding roads along the low, green-grassed Atlantic coast, you'll eventually come to the main town of Campbeltown. At one time, in the mid 19th century, there were about thirty distilleries here and a colliery, which meant that the area had the kingdom's highest GDP per capita. Today, Campbeltown is a quiet rural area, with only a few clues remaining of its glory days, such as a couple of grand but somewhat shabby hotels. The decline of the area, in any event in terms of whisky, reached its lowest point around the recent turn of the century. For a time, Campbeltown wasn't even a separate whisky region, despite being known in former times as "the Whisky Capital of the World." Now, however, the situation has improved. The Springbank and Glen Scotia distilleries were joined a few years ago by the restored Glengyle distillery. Reputable brands are shipped out from here, with everything from the fruity, triple-distilled whiskies such as Hazelburn and the exceptionally flavorsome two-and-a-half-times-distilled Springbank to the charmingly coarse and salt-splashed Glen Scotia. This is an area appreciated by enthusiasts but a little underestimated by the masses. Perhaps that's a good thing for the enthusiasts?

Longrow™

SINGLE MALT SCOTCH WHISKY

14 YEARS OLD

Cask type: 11 years in Refill Bourbon Casks

3 years in Fresh Burgundy Casks

Distilled: February 1997

Bottled: October 2011

Outturn: 7800 Bottles

Contents: 70cl Strength: 56.1%vol

PRODUCT OF SCOTLAND - SELECTED BY

Gavin McLachlan

Distillery Manager

J. & A. Mitchell & Co. Ltd.
Springbank Distillery · Campbeltown · Scotland

BURGUNDY WOOD

LONGROW
WOOD EXPRESSION

The Second World War

Roosevelt lifted the ban on alcohol on December 5, 1933. The whisky industry recovered, and recovery was quickest for those producers who had laid in stock and could realize their capital by starting to sell again immediately. Happiness was shortlived; with the outbreak of war in 1939, a trade embargo and submarines again caused a loss of momentum. The war was, however, very significant for the marketing of whisky in that Britain's involvement meant products were distributed further afield. The presence of American soldiers in Britain was also an important factor for awareness of Scottish whisky.

During the war, the whisky industry operated below capacity for reasons that included the rationing of raw materials for food and lack of manpower. The war meant that production of luxury items such as whisky had to be sacrificed. Some distilleries had a role in the conflict, however, and contributed to the war effort by producing yeast for foodstuffs, alcohol for fuel and acetone for explosives. There are also examples of distilleries who assisted by providing a roof over the head of soldiers as well as housing the production of mines.

We should mention in conclusion the group then known as Distillers Company Limited, DCL, and which later became a part of Diageo, as the company was an important player in the work to preserve the whisky industry and to manage pragmatically both the extreme demands of war and the setback caused by prohibition in the US.

The post-war period

When the war was over, the whisky industry and whisky drinkers also had to contribute to the rebuilding of Britain's economy. A tentative start gradually evolved into a strong upturn. In 1957, the first new distillery since 1900 was built, in Glen Keith.

In the 1960s there was an upswing, the like of which hadn't been seen since the reign of Queen Victoria.

New distilleries started up, existing ones increased their capacity and those that had gone to sleep were revitalized.

The upward trend slackened from the beginning of the 1970s, in the wake of the oil crisis and the recession that resulted. VAT—Value Added Tax—was raised in Britain. Tastes changed. During the happy hour of the 1980s stock market boom, sales of matured liquor fell badly and people took to drinking cocktails, clear spirits and bubbly. White wine broke into the market as an odd sort of healthy drinking option, despite the fact that a glass of wine contains more alcohol than a normal serving of whisky.

In the attempts to adapt to the new environment, distilleries were mothballed or closed down completely in one or two heavy swings of the scythe at the beginning of the 1980s. Where there had been 117 malt whisky distilleries at the beginning of the 1970s, after 1985 the number was down to about 80. This downsizing was thought necessary because total whisky sales dropped about 20% between 1978 and 1983. In the case of Ireland, that former whisky superpower, a market share of over 60% at the beginning of the 19th century had collapsed to a mere 2% in 1960. The number of distilleries had plummeted from about thirty in the mid 19th century to a pitiful two at the beginning of the 1970s.

Right now, having seen some six hundred years of history, whisky looks to have a bright future. In what we

> "[We see] changing attitudes and tastes—the rising tide of brown spirit demand is lifting all ships."
>
> John J Teeling, chairman of the Board and founder of the Cooley Distillery in Ireland, 2008.

might see as a post-material age, it seems the sensory experience and tradition that malt whisky offers are highly valued. That is suggested not least by the sales figures. During the 1990s, malt whisky doubled its proportion of total whisky sales. From being a marginal product, it now comprises around ten percent of the world whisky market. This figure is higher in some countries, for example in Sweden, where malt whisky is about a fifth of the total whisky sold.

The trend towards malt whisky really took off towards the end of the 1980s. To a certain extent it was catapulted into being by whisky producers in desperation. In the middle of this decade of bubbly, they took on board the ostentatiousness of the time and began to recast whisky as an exclusive drink of cachet and quality. Whisky was portrayed once again as fine liquor. And it really was a flying start. The interest sparked around malt whisky has brought about a fair wind worldwide for matured liquor in general.

Scottish, Irish, American, and Japanese whisky have now emerged as top sellers of high quality. As a result, production capacity has increased. This can be seen both at the small-scale exclusive end of the market and also in extreme examples such as market dominator Diageo's malt whisky distillery in Roseisle in Scotland. At one stroke, the new plant increased the company's capacity by a whole 10% to around 29 million gallons (around 110 million liters) annually.

After twenty or thirty years of whisky boom, the sales figures are still on a pleasing upward trend. In some markets, for example in Asia, Eastern Europe and South America, sales increases in double figures have on occasion been reported. Prosperous independent bottlers and private individuals have bought out group-owned distilleries. Distilleries that are now independent include Bruichladdich, Bladnoch, Benromach, and Glengoyne. In summary, despite a perceptible slowdown in the upward sales curve, the

expansion in recent decades has led to a greater and lasting consumption of, and interest in, whisky. What is most gratifying is that the enduring aspect of this seems to be a sophistication or a selectiveness on the part of the consumer, rather than a desire for indiscriminate consumption of volume. Not that volume doesn't sometimes have its place too, but I would like to suggest that, for whisky today, it would seem that quality has won over quantity.

S AND SPIRITS, FOR SEASON

FEINTS AND SPIRITS

Number of Gallons Bulk	Temperature	Indication	Strength	Number of Gallons Proof	Charge	
92						
3	63					
	66	113.2	21.1			
	68	44.11				
	69	113.6	18.7	1080.2		
83	114.6	19.1	870.0	3231.4	39	
90	348.8	174.4	610.9			
	348.8	67.11	591.6			
	348.8	63.6	368.6			

HISTORY IN CHRONOLOGICAL ORDER

The history of whisky is a story of alchemists, cantankerous Scots, settlers and inquisitive entrepreneurs with a liking for liquor. The following are some milestones from antiquity through to today, mostly relating to whisky, whiskey, or bourbon.

3000 BC: The ancient Egyptians get the hang of how heating and condensing increases the concentration of a liquid and can also separate mixtures of liquids.

800 BC: Distillation of arrack is known in India. Around this time distillation is also known in China.

384 BC: Aristotle is born (384–322); he later describes distillation in his Meteorologica.

432 AD: St. Patrick is sent to Ireland from France to convert the island to Christianity and is said also to have taught the art of distillation.

12th century: At the medical school in Salerno the use of distilled wine is first documented in Europe.

1170s: Henry II of England sends soldiers to Ireland. It's likely they brought uisge beatha home with them.

1494: Aqua vitae is first mentioned in writing when the monk John Cor buys 2,600 pounds of malt.

1506: Note from English King Henry VII's treasurer that the king bought "aqua vitae to the King" on his visit to Inverness, September 15 and 17.

1519: Hieronymus Braunschweig's book "Das Buch zu destillieren" is published. It describes with copious illustrations and much detail how brandywine is distilled for medicinal purposes.

1579: First reference in law to aqua vitae in Scotland. A grain shortage means production of aqua vitae is restricted to the upper classes.

1618: One of the first written references to the expression "uiskie". It's mentioned in the accounts after the funeral of an estate owner in the Highlands.

1644: Scottish parliament approves a proposed law to start taxing "everie pynt of aquavytie or strong watteris sold within the country." Tax on "strong watteris" for the first time. Taxation is to bring in money for the rebels against Charles I.

1690: The first distillery in Ferintosh is renamed after being burned down by the Jacobites while the owner Duncan Forbes of Culloden was fighting for King William II against James I in 1689. Forbes and his descendants are exempted from liquor tax, so-called excise duty, due to his efforts.

1707: The Union Treaty this year saw the combining of the Scottish and English parliaments.

1724–25: A malt tax is introduced in Scotland and simmering discontent erupts into illegal distilling, riots—the Shawfields Riots in Glasgow—smuggling and tax evasion.

1746: April 16, Catholic troops and clan militias are defeated under Bonnie Prince Charlie at Culloden. In this last battle on the British Isles, the Stuart family and the clans are swept away for good by a government army superior in both number and equipment.

1749: Giacomo Justerini arrives in London from Italy and sets up as a wine merchant in the firm Johnson & Justerini.

Mid 18th century: Unflavored whisky—"plain malt"— starts increasingly to part company with the flavored version. This happens more and more as quality improves and the flavoring is not needed to hide fusel oil, taints and bad craftsmanship.

1755: Lexicographer Samuel Johnson includes the word "whisky" in his dictionary dating from this year.

1779: Johnson & Justerini start to sell Scottish whisky.

1781: Distilling for domestic use is banned in Scotland.

1783: USA: Evan Williams starts up his distillery by the Ohio River in Louisville. He is the first person to be documented as distilling liquor in Kentucky.

1784: For tax reasons, the Wash Act establishes a dividing line in Scotland between the Lowlands and the Highlands—the Highland Line—between Greenock outside Glasgow, Perth and Dundee, south of Aberdeen.

1795: USA: Jacob Böhm sells his first whisky cask, having already started distilling in 1788 in Nelson County, Kentucky. Today, seven generations later, Jim Beam is one of the world's largest liquor producers. His descendant Fred B. Noe III is a whiskey ambassador for Jim Beam Bourbon.

1798: USA: According to legend, Elijah Craig discovers that wooden casks that have been more heavily charred inside give the whisky more taste and color. This is sometimes reported as having happened as early as 1789.

1805: USA: The original Grist Mill Distillery is founded, just outside Loretto. It is later to become Maker's Mark Distillery.

1812: USA: Elijah Pepper builds his distillery in Glenn's Creek, outside Versailles. Here, Dr. James Crow is to work as master distiller and it is here that he develops the sour mash principle to the full. Later it becomes the place where Woodford Reserve is produced.

1814: Pot stills holding less than 600 gallons (2.3 cubic meters) are banned in the Highlands, which in practice means a complete ban on whisky production locally. Matthew Gloag sets up his wholesale business in Perth, Matthew Gloag & Son.

1815: George Smith's illegal distillery in Drumin in Glenlivet produces high-quality whisky with a capacity of one hogshead per week. The distillery is considered at that time to be one of the best.

1816: Small Stills Act: Smaller stills and weaker wash are permitted throughout Scotland. First step towards abolition of tax differentials between Lowlands and Highlands. The number of legal distilleries more than triples within three years.

1820: John Walker starts his business as a licensed wholesaler in Kilmarnock.

1822: The distinction between the Highlands and the Lowlands in terms of taxation is removed and the penalty for illegal distilling is increased.

1823: A new tax law is enacted. The law includes changes in fee levels and the minimum still volume is reduced to 48 gallons (200 liters). In addition, it prescribes severe penalties for those caught distilling illegally or smuggling.

1823: USA: The sour mash process is invented by the Scottish liquor producer Dr. James Crow in Kentucky. He discovers that the yeast does better and the taste has consistency if he takes the bottom portion of the first distillation to cultivate the next batch of yeast.

1824: On the strength of the new tax law, George Smith takes out the first distillery license. Glenlivet in Minmore becomes the first legal distillery under the new legislation. Production of legal whisky now increases rapidly. By the end of 1825 there are already 263 licensed distilleries in Scotland—the 1823 law was the final blow for illegal distilling.

1825: USA: Alfred Eaton starts to produce whiskey at the place where Jack Daniel will later operate a distillery. Eaton is the first to charcoal filter his whiskey in the way that is characteristic of Tennessee whiskey.

1826: Robert Stein, of the Haig family, patents his column still, a forerunner of the continuous distillation still.

1827: George Ballantine starts his wholesale and wine business.

1830: Aeneas Coffey patents an improved version of the continuous still. The fact that he is Irish-born and a former tax inspector doesn't restrain him. The same principle is in use in industrial liquor distillation even today.

1831: Alfred Brooks buys the firm Johnson & Justerini and renames it Justerini and Brooks. The headquarters of the business is in London.

1834: John Philp & Co install the first Coffey still to be built at the Grange Distillery in Alloa, Clackmannanshire. By 2012 there are six column distilleries remaining in Scotland.

1837: Arthur Bell joins forces with T. R. Sandeman in Perth and later takes over the company's business.

ca. 1840: Whisky maturation in accordance with systematic modern methods commences.

1846: John Dewar starts his wine business in Perth.

1849: USA: Jasper "Jack" Newton Daniel is born. Fourteen years later he takes over Reverend Dan Call's distillery whose distillery manager, a slave called Nearest Green, has educated Jack in the art of distilling.

1853: Edinburgh entrepreneur Andrew Usher Jr. and his associates are the first to create and sell a blend of different types of whisky, a vatted malt. This concept is instrumental in blended whisky starting its triumphal march the following decade.

1858: A ship with aphid-infested vines from the US arrives at Bordeaux in France. An epidemic starts to rage, wiping out large parts of the European wine industry. The Rhône Valley is attacked in 1863, and the wine industry, and later the brandy industry, are badly affected.

1863: John Dewar is the first to sell whisky as branded goods, bottled and with paper labels. Today, Dewar's is still one of the Scottish whiskies that sells best on the other side of the Atlantic.

1866: USA: Jack Daniel is one of the first to register a distillery.

1867: Alexander Walker registers as a trademark the angled label still used today.

1872: The *Phylloxera vastatrix* wine aphid arrives in Charente, France, via carelessly-imported vines from the US. This now destroys sources of raw materials for cognac too, giving whisky welcome room for maneuver.

1877: Six grain distilleries in the Lowlands form The Distillers Company Ltd., DCL, the continuation of a trade association begun in 1865. Even if changed in all but name, the company comes to dominate the industry to this day.

1880: John Walker opens his London office. The son of George Smith, John Gordon Smith (of Gordon's Gin) enters into a legal battle for the name Glenlivet. The outcome is that other distilleries may only use the renowned Glenlivet as an addition to their own distillery name.

1880s: Export companies such as Wright & Greig, Robert Hillcoat & Sons, and Greenlees Brothers sell increasing amounts of blended whisky, including brands such as Famous Grouse and White Horse, as well as pure malt whisky in its own right, e.g. The Glenlivet, Caol Ila, Springbank, Bowmore, Dalmore, and Glenglassaugh.

1898: The dominant blending and distillery operator Pattison, Elder and Co. collapses, taking the whole whisky industry down with it in a major economic crisis.

1904: USA: The bottle becomes widely accepted for liquor packaging, after Michael J Owens' invention of an automatic bottling machine the previous year.

1909: After 37 meetings and cross-examination of 116 witnesses, it is determined that malt distillate from both pot and column still distillation can be called "whisky." At the same time this becomes part of the Whisky Act which goes through that year.

1909: Johnnie Walker Red, Black, and White Label are launched. Another milestone for marketing is reached this year when Tom Browne designs the purposeful Johnnie Walker man, "Still Going Strong," which is launched the following year.

1913: William M Bergius of Teacher's, William Teacher's grandson, invents the resealable cork.

1916: The Whisky Act is clarified by the addition of the requirement for a maturation period of at least three years.

1920: USA: On January 12 at 12:00 midnight, prohibition begins in the US, pushed through by the Republican teetotaler Volstead against President Woodrow Wilson's veto. (Incidentally, Volstead was of Norwegian descent.)

1924: Japan: Suntory starts producing whisky.

1925: White Horse Distillers launch the metal screwcap.

1929: Japan: Suntory's first product, Shirofuda (white label) is launched and sales are so poor that as an emergency solution they start to sell it for export a few years later.

1932: Bill Smith Grant, grandson of George Smith, the founder of Glenlivet, launches Glenlivet as a single malt.

1933: The alcohol ban in the US is lifted in December, with the words "What America needs now is a drink!" from President Roosevelt.

1934: Japan: Dai Nippon Kaju Kabushiki Kaisha, translated as The Great Japan Juice Company Ltd and later shortened to Nikka, is founded. The first whisky is launched in 1940.

1935: USA: The law that requires the use of new casks is adopted. The proposal comes from Senator Wilbur Mills from Arkansas, which is heavily forested with oak trees.

1961: USA: Minnesota is the last whole state to abolish the liquor ban.

1962: Brothers Charles and Sandy Grant decide to start exporting pot still whisky from Glenfiddich. The decision sets the ball rolling for the selling of single malt on a massive scale. At the time of the launch, eight-year-old Glenfiddich was sold as "straight malt" in the green, triangular bottle designed by the German Hans Schleger that is still used today.

1964: USA: Rules determining what may be called Bourbon become American law in Congress.

1966: Ireland: Irish Distillers Group is formed from Cork Distillers, Jameson and Powers.

1973: Britain joins the EEC and tax on whisky is reduced for the first time since 1896.

1975: Ireland: Irish Distillers' newly-built distillery is inaugurated, alongside the old one in Midleton.

1979–1980: Macallan initiates the campaign which is to put the distillery on the whisky map. Their slogan is "The nectar of the gods," with fat little angels who approve of Macallan. It's the first serious attempt to sell this now so established single malt.

1983: As a result of the recession following the oil crisis, DCL closes eleven of its forty-five distilleries (Banff, Benromach, Brora, Dallas Dhu, Glen Albyn, Glenochy, Glen Mhor, North Port, Knockdhu, Port Ellen, and St Magdalene).

1984: Blanton's launches as the first small batch whisky, bottled from hand-picked casks.

1985: Guinness acquires Arthur Bell & Sons, and the following year also DCL.

1986: USA: Heaven Hill introduces Elijah Craig 12-Year-Old, which they refer to as the original small batch whisky.

1987: Scotland's biggest malt distillery, Tomatin, is the first Scottish distillery to be bought up by a Japanese company, Takara Shuzo & Okura & Co Ltd.

1987: DCL and Arthur Bell & Sons Plc. combine to form United Distillers Plc., with head office in London.

1987: United Distillers launch their Classic Malts series with Cragganmore (Speyside), Lagavulin (Islay), Dalwhinnie (Highland), Oban (Western Highland), Talisker (Isles), and Glenkinchie (Lowlands).

1987: Ireland: Irish Distillers is sold to Pernod Ricard and John J Teeling, who is unsuccessful in the contest, founds the Cooley Distillery.

1988: USA: Through Booker Noe, Jim Beam launches "Booker's" as a Christmas present for its retailers. It becomes so popular that the following year it is made available as a retail product in its own right.

1992: USA: Brown-Forman buy back the distillery in Versailles and, after a praiseworthy and thorough renovation costing tens of millions of dollars, start to produce Woodford Reserve there.

1997: On May 12 the merger of two giants in the liquor industry is made public. The Guinness group's liquor division United Distillers merges with International Distillers & Vintners, the beverages section of food group Grand Metropolitan. The new group is called Diageo Plc. Amongst the company's whisky brands are the Classic Malts series, Johnnie Walker, J&B and Bell's.

1999: Sweden: In December of this year, Mackmyra is established as Sweden's first malt whisky distillery. The first volume product, Den Första Utgåvan (The First Edition), was launched in April 2008. Still young, but well made.

2000: USA: Brown-Forman buy a 50% equity stake in Finlandia and a 10% stake in Glenmorangie.

2004: Macallan launches the Fine Oak mixed-cask series as a complement to the sherry-matured whisky that has been the strict focus of its production to date.

2005: Kilchoman Distillery begins operations and thereby becomes Scotland's westernmost and Islay's eighth working distillery, on the far west side of the island. The whisky is launched in September 2009.

2006: Ireland: Pernod Ricard is forced to sell off Bushmills to Diageo on competition grounds.

2007: Ireland: Kilbeggan, the world's oldest distillery still with a valid license, becomes operational again on March 19 this year. The director of the drama is Cooley's and the first act began back in 1759.

2009: In spring this year, Diageo's new distillery Roseisle starts up with 14 stills. The whisky is to be used primarily in the company's blends.

2010: William Grant & Sons buy Tullamore Dew and start to discuss plans for a new Irish whiskey distillery. The same year they also buy the Hudson Whiskey trademark in order to distribute for the small New York-based distillery founded only in 2003.

2010: The classic Cutty Sark this year moves to Edrington Group, in exchange for Berry Brothers taking over Glenrothes.

2011: Edrington Group sell the Tamdhu Distillery, threatened with closure, to Ian Macleod Distillers.

Ireland

"Any of the girls who want something Irish in them?"

Anyone who knows their Thin Lizzy will recognize the words in the heading from a live performance in the late 1970s. They came, with a crooked grin, from one of the rock world's more contradictory characters—Phil Lynott, an Irishman of mixed race, in revealingly tight leather trousers and a haircut not unlike a bearskin hat. A moment earlier, he had been wondering if any of the girls in the audience had any Irish in them. Which he then followed up with the above offer. Setting aside the innuendo, getting on for forty years later it seems clear: both the girls in the audience and everyone else these days *do* get something Irish in them pretty often, to judge by the success of Irish whiskey sales.

Revenge is brewing: amber tumblers cupped in coarse craftsmen's hands in rural pub settings; commercials with flying houses in fantastic tales from the Irish countryside; massive campaigns and a stream of product launches—profile-raising is underway, and everything suggests that it is having an effect on the popularity of Irish whiskey. It must be due some acclaim anyhow; surely the kilt-wearing Scots and the bandy-legged Americans can't be the only ones on the whiskey map? If we start from media profile, Ireland has a pretty familiar image too. You're probably thinking of rolling green hills, a roaring swell, and perhaps a stone house with a pub at the roadside in a small village? By all means, spice up the picture with grim Northern Irish 70s realism—rough English policemen on the hunt for nimble-fingered bombers and troublemakers. Dilute with a couple of pints of Guinness in a gloomy bar and consume the mixture in the company of an Irish setter, and there you have an emerald-green dish of well-rooted national identity which is at least as sharply defined as Scotland's. Ironically enough, the Irish like the Scots have a national pride catalyzed by an unwillingness to be cowed by the same English supremacy; in both cases whiskey is one of the basic ingredients and for Ireland it's a whiskey that has now come in from the wilderness. Those of us on the padded side of the bar have now again realized that the amber liquid from the emerald isle deserves better than being drowned in sweetened coffee dripping with cream.

From the beginning

It's likely that the Irish learned the art of distilling liquor before the knowledge had reached Scotland—something to be voiced discreetly if there are any Scots in the vicinity. However, the fact that Ireland was converted to Christianity before Scotland is a strong indicator that the art of distillation arrived earlier in Ireland too. It was probably returning pilgrims who passed on the knowledge, although this may have not happened as early as in the time of St. Patrick as some people have asserted. Ireland's history has been intertwined with Scotland's since early times. The Dál Riata kingdom was established in the 5th century in the north east of what is now Ireland and what later became south west Scotland. This part of Europe became Christian at the beginning of the

6th century, and Christianity came from Ireland and spread to the north east.

It was much later that the Irish whiskey industry blossomed, at first on a small scale and later in larger operations. It is a recognized fact that, historically, Ireland dominated whiskey production right up to the late 19th century; if someone said "whiskey," it was Ireland you thought of.

In around 1750, there were about a thousand whiskey producers in Ireland. From the late 18th century onwards, Ireland enjoyed a steadily rising economy. For a lengthy period from the late 1700s onwards, Dublin was the Empire's second city. In 1830, Ireland had a population of around nine million, compared with approximately five million today. The Irish whiskey industry experienced good levels of growth up until the First World War. However, there was a real blip in the curve in 1845 when there was a drastic failure of the potato harvest. This had enormous

consequences in the form of typhus and cholera, resulting tragically in around a million deaths from starvation and disease.

Another development that was of interest in terms of whiskey, though dull in itself, was excise duty. A tax on malted barley was introduced in 1785, and remained in place until 1880. The tax brought about a change in the way the Irish select the raw materials for their whiskey which has lasted to this day. The new levy made whiskey made with 100% malted barley expensive. The producers therefore avoided barley

"Of all the wines of the world, Irish spirit is the best."

Czar Peter the Great on Irish whiskey, as early as 1682.

malt as far as possible, and replaced it with virgin barley, or other types of grain, in an attempt to keep margins high and taxation low.

The decline—pride goes before a fall

For the most part, Irish whiskey did extremely well during the 18th and 19th centuries due mainly to the domestic market. The producers became plump and contented thanks to the thirst of their fellow countrymen. There was a good deal of money to be made in Ireland alone, and the producers were therefore only moderately interested in exporting. This was to have repercussions further down the line. Ireland's share of the world market would go from 60% in 1830 down to 35% in 1900, and decline further until it was in its death throes at 2% in 1960. The industry that consisted of 28 distilleries in 1886 imploded, so

that twenty years later there were only four, and then a mere two by the 1970s. This, then, was the situation before the Irish came to their senses, started to cooperate and got seriously down to work. There's a little more on the historical background to this below.

In around 1730, the volume of taxed whiskey was about 185,000 gallons (about 700 cubic meters). It shot up to just under 4.5 million gallons (17,000 cubic meters) in 1795 and to a whole 7.5 million gallons (29,000 cubic meters) in 1811. Demand fairly exploded. Although exports were increasing, sales were mainly to the domestic market, as noted previously.

In addition to their self-sufficient attitude, the Irish were convinced that the pot still method was the right way and the only way to make whiskey. The launch of the column still in the 1830s came to be something the Scots concerned themselves with, and the western part of the kingdom resisted, calling the

pure and understated grain whisky "silent whiskey". The divergence in the manufacturing philosophies of Scotland and Ireland that now began was reinforced by the law change in 1909 which ruled that the raw liquor produced in column stills and blended with malt whisky could also be called whisky. Productivity in the Scottish whisky industry increased, while the Irish clung on to their pot stills and struggled on using only the inefficient batch distillation process.

You might ask whether this confirms the prejudice about obstinate Irishmen who go their own merry way against better judgment? Possibly, but let's add some balance to the picture. There was product development as early as the 19th century, and also a wide range of goods. There were many more distilleries than there are today, and levels of production were high even by modern standards. For example, in around 1870 the old Midleton distillery was producing no fewer than 660,000 gallons (2.5 million liters) of raw liquor per

year. During the interwar period, production declined steeply and the new distillery didn't achieve this level of annual volume again until 1974–1975. Productivity was considerably higher than in Scotland. Figures from the late 1880s show that the 28 distilleries then operating in Ireland were producing just under 12 million gallons (45,000 cubic meters), while 129 Scottish distilleries were only producing 21.5 million gallons (82,000 cubic meters) despite the fact they were much greater in number.

On the subject of taste, Irish whiskey from the northern parts of the island had distinct smoky elements due to the use of peat when kilning. The triple distillation that is considered so typically Irish is also counterbalanced by a number of double-distilling whiskey producers. This is amongst the details recorded by the journalist Alfred Barnard in *Distilleries of the United Kingdom* in which he documents the British whisky industry of the 1880s. He also makes another

interesting observation on the low percentage of malted barley and the fact that grain other than barley is sometimes used, not just in those column distilleries that process corn and wheat. Two of these differences in production that influence taste, i.e. the use of unmalted barley and triple distillation, have persisted to this day and are for many people the distinctive features of Irish whiskey.

That the Irish were willing to develop their product was also clear from their readiness to allow their whiskey to mature. As early as the 1870s there is evidence that systematic maturation was carried out purely for reasons of taste. Contributing to this in no small way was the fact that Dublin and Cork were, with Bristol, amongst the most important locations for the large-scale import and bottling of sherry. Added to this, the whiskey industry, despite being saturated, was actually given a boost in the mid 1870s when the vine aphid put a temporary stop to cognac production.

These are a series of factors that give a more nuanced picture of Irish whiskey producers. Looking at these, it does seem that they were a little more on the ball than is often considered to be the case. All the product variations mentioned above should have had a positive effect on the consumer's experience of whiskey and the range of goods available. What was hampering the industry, however, was that there was only limited choice. In a bar or in a liquor store, while at best you might be able to choose between one whiskey and another, at worst you might only have a choice between whiskey, gin or brandy.

Despite some willingness to innovate and a few, creative, individual producers, external factors nevertheless descended like the proverbial wet blanket over a heated whiskey industry; there followed a rapid cooling and a gasping breath as the last bit of air escaped. At the beginning of the 20th century, the domestic-oriented economy went into a severe recession.

The effect was intensified by the long-simmering discontent with the English which was growing into increasingly heated confrontations. Self-government for the Irish was also being advocated in political circles but didn't come about until 1914. Autonomy was short-lived, however, as it was superseded when war broke out and also when the nationalists took up the armed struggle. In 1916 things heated up even more with the Easter Rising. It was put down after five days, but had direct consequences for the whiskey producers as an embargo was imposed on exports to the Empire in order to suppress the Irish struggle for freedom. This did not, however, extinguish the spark that had been ignited. In 1921, the Irish Free State was established.

The instability and the conflicts that had occurred, and which followed in the young nation too, came as the first little stroke that would fell the great oak. The oak itself was swaying dramatically, since one of the consequences of emancipation was severely reduced exports to the rest of Britain.

The above-mentioned embargo also hit hard as it meant that exports to other parts of the world were seriously reduced. All too soon, the train derailed completely. Prohibition in the US from 1920 to 1933 took its toll a couple of years into the 1920s. Established trading contacts in the US could no longer be utilized. Export volumes plummeted. The fact that an enormous market had disappeared over-night left the entire whiskey industry at a loss.

Ireland's reputation was also dragged through the mud by illegal cellar bars all over the US, the so-called speakeasies. These served home-distilled liquor, which they often advertised as Irish whiskey; this of course pulled the rug out from under the feet of the real Irish whiskey.

The client base of this still innovation-averse industry was gradually wiped out. The Scots' habit of exporting saved their sales despite the American ban; this was partly also because they indirectly defied the ban and exported to the people who smuggled their whisky into the US. Meanwhile, the Irish, like law-abiding country cousins, could only look on as they were increasingly outpaced by tartan-checkered, sophisticated, whisky floggers. Irish stocks sold out and the producers were as if paralyzed, unable to produce new goods on the same scale.

The only light in the darkness was the determination of the larger, wealthy Irish families to survive. The Jamesons and the Murphys spearheaded the effort to gather up what was left of earlier whiskey production. What they accumulated would later come to form the basis of Irish Distillers and thus of today's growing and flourishing industry.

A lost generation

Emancipation and prohibition were unquestionably disastrous for the whiskey industry, as can clearly be seen from the export figures below. Clearly, too, the industry didn't recover until several decades later, in the 1960s. What also happened at that time is that production using the pot still was abandoned and Paddy, Jameson, Powers, and several others changed from what was called pure pot still whiskey to blended whiskey in line with the model that had been so successful for the Scots.

Year	Export (US gallons per year)	Export (Liters per year)
1925	694,078	2 627 372
1935	87	331 576
1945	74	280 363
1955	96	364 488
1965	206	780 703

(Source: *Irish whiskey* by E. B. McGuire, with thanks to Barry Crockett.)

In the Japanese manner

Like the young Irish republic, Irish whiskey has experienced both misery and stagnation as well as the acclaim and sales success of more recent times. Those producers who had survived prohibition and the war engaged in a fierce battle with each other during the post-war period. However, there were a couple of events which saw the embittered competitors able to back off and join forces in order to survive. Firstly, the Cork Distillers group was formed, and in 1966 this merged with Powers and Jameson to become the Irish Distillers Group. Then, in 1974, a monopoly was created in the Irish whiskey industry when Seagrams sold Bushmills to Irish Distillers.

The crisis in the whisky sector that affected both Ireland and Scotland badly during the 1970s and 1980s meant that the Irish too were forced to take some drastic measures as part of their overhaul of existing production resources. The group that had been formed therefore invested in a new, giant, distillery, which was completed in 1975, standing alongside the old distillery in Midleton.

Similar to the Japanese, they chose to construct the manufacturing facility to make it possible to produce many different types of whiskey in one location. In Midleton's case, this is achieved through a combination of column distillation and pot stills. The common denominator for the brands mentioned above is that they all have an element of liquor from pot stills, with or without neutral grain spirits depending on the whiskey in question. The liquor from pot stills is distilled three times and the raw material is about 60% unmalted barley. The use of unmalted barley has its roots in history through the malt tax that was introduced in 1785, as we have seen previously. Today the Irish still make their whiskey with a mixture of both unmalted and malted barley, even if the taxation level for both is now much the same.

The column distillation method chosen for the new distillery at Midleton is called the extractive distillation system. The process is based on a Canadian model. Distillation takes place in three stages using what are called the beer, extractive and rectifying stills respectively. The result is a mild, sweet whiskey which is reminiscent of the neutral Canadian whisky, and there are also parallels with the taste of the best-selling, smooth, Cuban rum products produced in column stills, e.g. Havana Club, and a number of others.

Bushmills is still in place in Northern Ireland, now owned by Diageo. The other brands mentioned are part of the Pernod Ricard product portfolio. Apart from its location and its owner, Bushmills also differs from other distilleries in that it uses malted barley to a much greater extent. One interesting historical note is that, in the northern parts of Ireland, there was a tradition which lasted into the 19th century of whiskey being made with smoked malt, presumably due

to proximity to the salty spray of the Atlantic. There are also one or two examples of this later, even into the 20th century.

Because Irish whiskey is relatively mild, the character of the cask has a prominent role to play. In both the Irish Republic and Northern Ireland there are examples of maturation taking place in several types of cask, such as Connemara which is put into sherry casks and the well-known Bushmills 16-year-old malt which matures in bourbon, sherry, and port casks. The bourbon cask character typical of Irish whiskey today is however a couple of decades younger than is the case for Scottish whisky. According to Barry Crockett, head of the distillery at Midleton, it wasn't until the 1960s that the bourbon cask came to dominate what was laid down to mature in the Irish warehouses.

A pick-me-up

After cooperation became the name of the game for the Irish from 1966 onwards, the decline leveled off and even became a shaky upturn. The weakening situation stabilized, largely because the plan to re-profile Jameson and other known brands had a positive outcome. Irish Distillers started to look so attractive that Pernod Ricard took them over in 1987. They did however have to pluck Bushmills out of the group in 2006 in favor of the whisky giant Diageo, seemingly so that Pernod Ricard would not be too dominant in Ireland.

The Pernod Ricard takeover brought about much improved distribution and sales administration for Irish Distillers. The Irish businessman John J Teeling had lost out on the Irish Distillers deal, but instead started Cooleys in 1987. It was the first new Irish distillery for a hundred years. Teeling's idea was supposedly to drive up profitability and increase sales and then sell at a profit to Pernod Ricard, but the plan was frustrated by the competition authorities.

By the turn of the millennium and beyond, the slight upturn discernible for Irish whiskey from the end of the 1980s had turned into a vigorous upswing. For the Midleton distillery, what was an annual volume of over 3 million gallons (12 million liters of raw liquor) in 1995 had by 2011 turned into no less than 8.7 million gallons (33 million liters), and that meant they had reached their production ceiling. An expansion is being planned to enable a possible annual volume of almost 17 million gallons (64 million liters). Added to this are the volumes produced by Bushmills and Cooleys, around 1.2 million gallons (4.5 million liters) and 900,000 gallons (3.3 million liters) respectively; 680,000 gallons (2.6 million liters) of the volume produced at Cooleys consists of grain whiskey. Ambitions to increase the volume of Jameson for export have been fulfilled with two-figure sales increases in markets such as South Africa, Russia and Eastern Europe. Single pot still whiskey is being launched and more and more vintages and different types of secondary aging are being specified over and above the familiar personalities on the Irish section of the whiskey shelves. The vision for the future is for the single pot still to become for Ireland what single malt already is for Scotland. The pot still will be the buzzword and the mark of quality. In the midst of these gratifying winds of change, it is the character of the whiskey that nonetheless remains as a fixed point in our lives. Irish whiskey is still what it always has been for most of us: softness, unmalted barley, tones of bourbon, apple, peach, pear, blackcurrant, and a little sauvignon blanc, with all the associations of cat pee and everything else that goes with it …

A bit of the Irish

The Irish have of course had the self-respect to enshrine their definitions of whiskey in law. They distinguish between three categories:

» Irish grain whiskey (column distillate)

» Irish pot still whiskey (made with either malted or unmalted barley)

» Irish malt (pot still whiskey made only with malted barley)

Note, however, that the law doesn't require triple distillation. As has been mentioned, Bushmills distills twice, and Cooley does the same in some cases. Traditionally it has been the triple distillate that has dominated, but the picture of Irish whiskey from the 19th century onwards is largely one of pot still distillation using both double and triple distillation, although with significant input from column distillation. The raw material has chiefly been unmalted barley, although barley malt has of course also been used, as well as, in earlier cases, other grain rich in starch such as corn, oats, and wheat.

USA

As a European, I find the United States fascinating. The country accommodates the full range of opinions and expression and harbors both extreme levels of luxury and ostentation as well as equally profound levels of poverty. It's true that media reporting is not always objective and neither is it comprehensive. However, the country that has produced the most Nobel Prize winners and is the world's largest democracy undoubtedly has its selling points. Media sales are of course driven by anything extreme or abnormal, and so reporting on the US in other countries very often focuses on this type of news. Any similarities between the US and Europe therefore suddenly become obvious. And I take pleasure in the similarities, as I go about in my respectable, perhaps sometimes colorless, everyday life, wearing my Converse sneakers and with my Levi's and my Jack Daniel's sweater on.

One of the similarities between the Western countries can be found in the way in which alcohol and its opponents have developed through history: we're talking here about heavy consumption, the temperance movement, illegal distilling and smuggling. You were thinking that applied to Europe? Yes—but to the USA as well. There are historical similarities and also more recent ones. One known difference between the US and many other countries we should mention is of course prohibition, but more about that later.

Another factor in common is that there is often underrated domestic liquor production, where the country's own inhabitants are far too unaware of its qualities. This ignorance about a country's domestic products can, however, be a delight for anyone attempting to educate the masses in the subject. It's perfectly possible to learn to appreciate Maker's Mark and Booker's. When producers and devoted consumers share the same desire to spread the gospel, you just have to join in, pour a glass and go along with it.

Exported craftsmanship

It's only a slight exaggeration to say that there was originally no difference between European and American whisky. The settlers who fled from religious enemies or poor harvests simply to survive took their knowledge of distilling with them. They were Scots, Irishmen, and Germans, who continued to make liquor for household requirements and sometimes a little more. Whiskey production in the US can be said to have started in 1733. In that year, the British government brought in a statutory tax on non-British molasses, in what was called the Molasses Act. This was a not insignificant factor in the events that later sparked the revolution. The soon-to-be Americans defied the British authorities and switched to buying molasses from the French or Spanish colonies, where it was in good supply. The 1733 Act led to some mild contempt of court, because people ignored the legislation, but also to organized smuggling.

The use of molasses as raw material was gradually abandoned. Production of rye whiskey started in Maryland and Pennsylvania where they made use of the surplus of rye to produce liquor. This meant that whiskey slowly replaced the molasses-based rum that had been predominant up until then. The change was complete after the revolution, when an embargo on molasses was imposed on the new USA. The molasses

trade that remained was also to a large degree dependent on the slave trade. When slavery was abolished, the decline of rum production accelerated further as the only way to get hold of both slaves and molasses after that point was through smuggling, a very risky affair.

The young American state needed money to finance the construction of its government structures. One source of income was a tax on whiskey production. This resulted in a rebellion. Thirteen thousand soldiers were sent to western Pennsylvania to put down the revolt amongst the settlers. They still refused to pay. President Washington therefore made the decision to suppress the rebels by sending troops to the troubled parts of the country. These events are known as "the Whiskey Rebellion" and took place from 1791 to 1794. It's worth noting in this context that George W himself had an interest in whiskey. A few years after the rebellion, he started his own distillery on his estate in Virginia.

Further unrest was averted by the president through various political decisions. These Scottish-Irish settlers offered stubborn resistance to the tax.

The well-known punishment of tarring and feathering designed to ridicule the victim—dipping someone into tar and rolling them in feathers—is said to have come about during this period of unrest. One or two people in authority are said to have been subjected to this as a result of their efforts to maintain

> "Civilization begins with distillation."
>
> William Faulkner (1897–1962), winner of the Nobel Prize for Literature in 1949

tax compliance. Bear this in mind the next time you read *Lucky Luke*. However, the state found a way to appease the distillers who refused to pay tax on their products. Thomas Jefferson, the Governor of Virginia, offered them sixty acres of land in Kentucky, then part of Virginia, if they established new settlements there. One of the requirements was that they should cultivate the "native corn" wherever they settled. Few families were able to use everything that this acreage produced. With an area of cultivated land about the size of fifty football pitches, there was a great risk of grain going to waste, and so the simple solution for the farmers was to make whiskey from the surplus. Another factor sometimes said to have contributed to the boom in whiskey production in these new settlements was freight: a horse could carry well over 200 pounds (about 100 kilos) of corn or rye in its raw form, but the equivalent of up to six times more once it had been converted into liquid form. In addition, there was an increase in the selling price of whiskey. This was killing several birds with one stone: the government presided over a country that was calm; the country was colonized; contented farmers didn't have to pay tax, and were not only well-fed, but also got whiskey and perhaps a little more out of their seed—what we today would call a win-win situation.

Kentucky, a new state with new whiskey habits

The French were of some assistance during the Revolutionary War against Britain. Certain parts of the country were also French colonies, and certain new parts of the US were therefore given French names. One example was the western part of Virginia, Kentucky County, which was divided into several parts in 1780 and 1786. One of the new parts was called Bourbon County after the French royal family.

In 1792, Kentucky became a federal state in its own right and Bourbon remained as one of its counties. It was at this time that bourbon whiskey came into being.

However, if we leave romanticism at the rinkside and get on with the match, we find that this type of whiskey is not an invention at all, it came about through sheer hard work. This period saw the gradual development of corn-based whiskey in well-charred maturation casks, thanks to interplay between producers and customers that in the end carved out a new tradition and a new type of whiskey. Bourbon-type whiskey emerged during the late 18th century. To begin with, it was given names such as Western whiskey and Kentucky whiskey.

Legend has it that the first person to distill on a commercial basis was called Evan Williams. He established his business up in Louisville in northern Kentucky. The invention of bourbon, however, is sometimes credited to pastor Elijah Craig. He is said to have launched his whiskey around 1789. It was matured for a little longer than normal because it was transported by raft from Louisville all the way down to New Orleans. The casks were also charred on the inside since the pastor didn't like their smell, as they had often contained fish or other goods for the previous owner. Because the whiskey took on color from the casks, it came to be known as *red liquor*.

There's another explanation of how whiskey came to be matured in charred casks featuring a tight-fisted cooper. When he was heating the oak staves so that he could bend them to make his casks, they caught fire, and instead of throwing the staves away he used them in the casks. This was a quality defect that would soon be shown to have benefits, since his casks gave the whiskey some completely unexpected and agreeable flavors.

Neither the cooper nor Rev. Craig were located in Bourbon County, however, so the background to

the name of the liquor is not completely clear. One common theory is that the whiskey from this area became popular and was therefore requested by the name of the county. The only real connection that can be proven in this context is that Kentucky has a county named after the French royal family, the Bourbons, and that in 1922 there was a whiskey produced there, called Bourbon. The first evidence that Bourbon County *was* a source of whiskey, even if its provenance is unclear, does, however, date back as far as 1787. In that year, James Garrad, later Governor of Kentucky, and two others, were accused by a court in Bourbon County of having sold liquor without a permit. And finally, here comes the ironic part: whiskey is no longer produced in the Bourbon County from which it gets its name.

Pure water, corn, and official whiskey

When the settlers moved to the west it was to the limestone belt that runs from Pennsylvania via Kentucky and Indiana down to the southern tip of Illinois. Here, the bedrock gave a pure water that was rich in minerals but free of iron. This was a prerequisite for good whiskey. Pure freshwater is no longer essential these days since we can now manipulate the chemistry of water as required. Nevertheless, more than three-quarters of US whiskey production is still located in this area. The development of the sour mash method also came about due to the mineral-rich, alkaline water. The yeast didn't work as well as the producers would have liked and so they used some of the liquid from the bottom of the still in the previous distillation in the next fermentation process. This process, which resembles the sourdough breadmaking method, made the wash sourer and the whiskey

producers happier. It also meant that each distillery could achieve consistency from fermentation to fermentation. The move to the south west also had consequences in terms of raw materials. Corn came to be used more and more in the warmer climate, and this brought considerable benefits as it was an economical crop, rich in starch and with a high yield.

About twenty years into the 19th century, Bourbon was the predominant name for the whiskey that was produced in Kentucky in accordance with methods similar to those of today. Bourbon is sometimes called "America's Native Spirit," and a resolution in Congress in 1964 declared bourbon to be the only official liquor of this young country. It must be pure coincidence that bourbon was recognized in law the same year that Keith Richards and buddies released their first album.

An unidentified, contented American, one of the inhabitants of the small town of Lynchburg. The setting is the veranda outside one of the shops in the town square, where you can hardly even buy a fishing rod that doesn't have a Jack Daniel's logo. Incidentally, the number of inhabitants was removed from the label in 2011; probably the right thing to do, considering that the centuries-old figure of 361 people is now six thousand plus!

Liquor producers and temperance zealots

From their initial trade in local markets, the producers expanded in line with capacity and demand. There were clear parallels with other consumer products and also with European whisky. Trademarks, packaging and distribution networks were developed. Producers familiar to us today set up in business: Jim Beam, Four Roses and Jack Daniel made their appearance and moved into the markets in new corners of the US and later also in other countries. Each company was keen to set itself apart so that it would get noticed in the general stores and also on the world market, and they achieved this through advertising and packaging aimed at the customer. The four-sided bottles of old Johnnie and Mr. Jack stand out to this day.

When the bottle was launched as packaging around the turn of the twentieth century, it ushered in a new era. Suddenly, it was a brand, a product with its own identity that was in demand. It was no longer just whiskey that was asked for in the general stores. Amongst the first pioneers in this area were the men behind the giant Brown-Forman group. George Garvin Brown, a promising, young pharmaceuticals salesman in Louisville, thought he had spotted a gap in the whiskey market. In 1870, Brown and his half-brother clubbed together to raise $5,000 and then then set about producing whiskey in bottles which were said to be of "medicinal standard".

Sour mash, nothing special

There's nothing special about American whiskey being produced using the sour mash method, since that's the way it's been done for almost two hundred years. The pure water is far too calcium-rich and alkaline for the yeast to work properly. The problem is solved by using a working method that resembles baking bread with sourdough. After distilling, the sour liquid at the bottom of the still, called the backset, is used for the next mashing. The process is started by adding yeast to the backset which then starts to grow. Once started, the yeast mixture is poured over the new mash. This gives a very active yeast culture and a lower pH value, and also ensures continuity in character from batch to batch. The person usually credited with having developed the sour mash method is a Scottish distiller in Kentucky, Dr. James Crow, who is said to have created the method in 1823.

This way of working, using sour mash, is today the only method that's used for all bourbon and also for Tennessee whiskey. Admittedly, some smaller craft distillers experiment with other methods, but this activity is very marginal. One difference between bourbon and Tennessee whiskey that's worth noting here is that, in Tennessee, producers take a larger portion of the new mash from the previous one. The process of distilling whiskey without using the previous distillation's backset, i.e. using sweet mash, disappeared in the 19th century and is no longer used on a major, commercial scale. Sweet mash gives a higher yield, but requires fresh yeast each time, which meant that historically the quality and character varied.

JACK DANIEL'S OLD NO 7

They say no-one knows why the world's best-known American whiskey is called Old No 7, and recent commercials include theories that show all the signs of having been invented over a whiskey in the marketing department. They include everything from Jack's seventh girlfriend to other, even more fanciful, romanticizations. There are lots of older theories too, although a couple of these also seem as groundless as a southern states swamp. If you visit Lynchburg and its distillery, note that every guide has his own explanation for the name "Old No 7" ...

Besides the ideas of the guides, there are also historians and others who have their own ideas. Any absolute certainty about the name disappeared one grey Monday, on October 9, 1911. That was the day old Jack died from the effects of gangrene, caused by a fit of rage directed at his safe. So now you have to judge for yourself which of the following is the truth:

» The distillery was building number seven along the river where it was first established. This explanation agrees to a certain extent with the next one.

» The founders Jack Daniel and Lem Motlow registered the distillery as number seven in the fourth district in Tennessee. The figure seven does subsequently feature on writing paper, casks, pitchers and stamps. When tax districts four and five were merged in 1876, the distillery was called number sixteen instead, despite the fact that no other distillery was renamed. From the marketing point of view this didn't work, as the number seven was already well-established in the minds of the customers. Jack and Lem therefore continued to sell their whiskey as "Old No 7". It's a very mundane but highly plausible theory about the origin of the name.

» The size of the bubbles in the raw whiskey should match the size of 7-gauge shot to be of the right strength. A theory about as sustainable as a bubble itself.

» Seven casks were mislaid during handling. When they were returned, Jack wrote "7" on the side of each cask and sold them. The tradesmen who tested it became ecstatic and asked Jack eagerly for more of "that old number seven". Even if they had rounded off with "please", this would seem to be a theory that's doctored in favor of the whiskey producer. Why did he write "7" on all seven of the casks? Was it usual for lost casks to be numbered? Was the diligent Jack Daniel really in the habit of losing casks?

» Jack got to know a Jewish trader with a chain of seven shops, and Jack believed there was magic in that number. Surely Jack was not a numerologist?

» It was the mash bill and the maturation that they arrived at by trial and error in the seventh mashing that was the best, and so this whiskey began to be sold as number seven. An explanation similar to that of VAT69. In the case of Jack's whiskey, this raises the question of what the other mash bills were? And, in any event, why "*Old* No 7"?

» At the time the whiskey was created, bachelor Jack had a number of lady friends. The one he had discreetly named number seven was his own favorite and therefore the favorite whiskey also got to be number seven. A valid theory, but only in a commercial.

The final theory comes from a reliable source and is without doubt the true one. So much became clear after a conversation with Roger Brashears at the Jack Daniel's distillery. After more than forty years at the distillery, Brashears was certain of his story—not least because he invented the theory himself in about 1970.

> *"'Y God, every day we make it, we're going to make it the best we can."*
>
> Jack Daniel

The temperance movement turns into gang violence

For many of the producers, the growing temperance movement was a major hindrance. Public opinion was growing against alcohol, primarily in the Bible Belt in the South where many of the production facilities were located. The free church immigrants who came to the US clustered for the most part in the Midwest and the South. It was there that the temperance movement developed as a reaction to the high level of alcohol consumption. The authorities took action too. They introduced taxes, and rules against home-distilling, against consumption in general, and also against better judgment. An example of the latter was the law that banned liquor within four miles of a school. Added to this were more practical campaigns. Temperance extremists vandalized bars and distilleries, and the teetotalers' activities did in fact result in a steadily increasing number of counties with an alcohol ban across the US. There was a strong lobby working for a total ban that also had the wind in its sails.

Free churchers, taxmen and fanatical women

The religious breakaway groups who fled from Europe to the new America flourished in their new homeland. Many of these faith groups were concentrated in the Midwest and South, in the areas where whiskey was produced. In their eyes, the Bible Belt lay right in the middle of the whiskey swamp. The rising consumption of alcohol and the consequences of that provoked a reaction from the church, and also from legislative bodies, at both a local and a federal level. The temperance movement in the US started to gain momentum from the early 19th century onwards. One not altogether surprising coincidence is that the emergence of bourbon as a distinct product is often dated to around the same time, i.e. from about the start of the 1820s.

The action taken against alcohol varied. For the authorities, the weapons were taxes and regulations. They hit whiskey pioneer Jack Daniel and in his case the offensive was personified by the former general, Green B. Raum. The general enlisted in the IRS in 1876 to combat alcohol and engaged in the fight against illegal—and in some cases even legal—distilleries in Tennessee. The illegal ones were targeted for penalties and tax registration, a strategy that was surprisingly successful. In certain districts, the number of legal distilleries tripled, with the pleasing result that tax revenue increased. As could be expected, this spurred the general on. The legal distilleries were scrutinized ever more zealously with the aim of uncovering illegal activity or deviation from the rules. The producers grew more and more irritated at the tax officers' and lawmakers' ignorance of the details of production. Rules and guidelines were drawn up without reference to actual differences in yield between sweet and sour mash processes. There was a requirement that every bushel of corn should produce 3 gallons of whiskey, despite the fact that the sour mash method only produced about 2.5. This may seem like minor detail, but there was a risk that the requirements could lead to the producers sacrificing quality by opting, for example, for a faster mashing stage. For the authorities, the aim of the rules was to get control, so that nothing that was produced could escape taxation. Consequently, fees and levies hit people unfairly purely due to ignorance, at what was additionally a time of recession.

> "The making of liquor is regarded as an honorable livelihood. If people are injured from the use of liquor, the injury arises not from the use of a bad thing but from the abuse of a very good thing."
>
> Abraham Lincoln (1809–1865)

E336852

R℞ Sp Frumente — KIND OF LIQUOR / QUANTITY / DIRECTIONS

FULL NAME OF PATIENT — Glennie Schnitter — DATE PRESCRIBED 12/13/31

PATIENTS ADDRESS — 920 N Taylor — NUMBER / STREET / CITY St Louis, Mo / STATE

PRESCRIBERS SIGNATURE — PRESCRIBERS PERMIT NUMBER — 14,700

PRESCRIBERS ADDRESS — 634 No. Grand St Louis, Mo — NUMBER / STREET / CITY / STATE

CANCELED — DRUG STORE NAME AS ON PERMIT — PERMIT NUMBER

DISPENSERS SIGNATURE — DATE FILLED AND CANCELED — STRIP STAMP NUMBER 215083-11

STORE ADDRESS 4130

Another way of clamping down on liquor was to introduce legislation on aspects of alcohol other than actual production. One example of this was the Four-Mile Law. The law was passed in the 1840s and tightened at the end of the 19th century. It meant that alcohol could not be produced or sold in smaller places (the line was drawn at 2,000 inhabitants from 1899) or within a radius of 4 miles from a school. There were of course ramifications that also affected those who had toed the line and paid their taxes. Both distilleries and sales outlets had to either close their doors or move.

Many of the authorities' regulations may justifiably be considered peculiar, in many cases substantiated by nothing more than plain ignorance. Despite that, the methods were nonetheless lawful. However, there were also unlawful methods—fanatical ones. Perhaps the best-known of all the shrieking temperance activists was Carry Nation. Carry, a striking (to say the least) lady in her fifties, claimed to be doing God's work by destroying bars wherever they were. Extremely embittered because of her alcoholic, late husband, she was on the warpath against anything relating to men, sex, smoking, alcohol and immoral vices. According to Carry, men were "nicotine-soaked, beer-besmirched, whiskey-greased, red-eyed devils." Oh well, she would have had no problem avoiding a couple of those vices with that sort of pick-up line.

She and her kindred spirits mounted raids on saloons in the South. Even pharmacists who had been selling cognac for medicinal purposes were subjected to something more akin to the Kristallnacht than alcohol education. Carry Nation stirred up mobs consisting mainly of women. Singing, and equipped with hatchets and zeal, they attacked bars in the South so that splinters flew. Their motive was that these branches of hell on earth were destroying mankind, and must therefore be put out of action by Mrs Nation and the Women's Christian Temperance Union. Yeehaa!

Prohibition in 1906

The temperance movement grew state by state and by 1906 an alcohol ban was already in force for as much as 40% of the US population. Geographically, this draining effect was centered on the north east. After the First World War, the National Prohibition Act of 1919—better known as the Volstead Act—was pushed through, with the assistance of propaganda about the evil Germans and their reputation as brewers and distillers, and also sententious moralizing from the temperance movement suggesting that the law was needed to save women, children and families.

In addition, the chairman of the Senate committee that drove the Prohibition Act, the Minnesotan tee-totaler Andrew Volstead managed to force it through against President Woodrow Wilson's veto. The law permitted an amendment to be made to the United States Constitution on alcohol prohibition—the Eighteenth Amendment. A total ban on alcoholic beverages containing more than 0.5% alcohol was introduced in the whole of the US with effect from January 16, 1920.

Despite the dangers attributed to alcohol, the effect of the ban was the opposite of what the prohibition zealots had believed and hoped would result from the new law. Consumption went sky high, albeit on the quiet. It was illegal to drink, produce and sell alcoholic drinks. Drinking often went on at speakeasies. Snappy adverts for alcohol were therefore forbidden. Instead, those who fared best were those who bribed the most and, worse still, those who benefited from the rattle emanating from Mr. Thompson. One clear consequence of the ban was that it destroyed the livelihood of those who had worked in the legal beer and liquor industries. Subcontractors such as coopers, bottle-makers, coppersmiths, and distributors all followed down into the abyss. It did, however, successfully provide a living for everyone who was outside

the law. And the benefits for alcohol policy? By 1930, consumption was six times what it had been when the ban was introduced.

"King of the bootleggers"

George Remus was a skillful businessman who, with his extensive network of speakeasies, was behind much of the organized, illegal selling and trading of alcoholic beverages. Remus had a noteworthy approach to solving family problems, and equally noteworthy methods of selling alcohol. He was known as king of the industry for good reason. With his knowledge of the law, he was able to exploit the loophole in the legislation on purchase and distribution of alcohol for medicinal use. Remus bought up both distilleries and drug companies and hit upon a symbiosis in prohibition whereby he could sell alcohol to his own drinking outlets on medical grounds.

One of George Remus's more spectacular coups involves Jack Daniel's. In June 1923, he bought 893 casks of whiskey there. By August he had already stolen the whiskey contained in them from himself. The casks were refilled with water to hide the theft, and it wasn't until a month later that the deception was discovered. By then, the owner had sold on the liquor illegally, having first diluted it by half with water, thus raking in two million dollars.

Violin cases and the death of distilleries

The total ban put the legal distilleries under great strain. Those whiskey producers who were quick to think and act managed to put supplies away for sale at a later date, but most of them had a very tough time. Many hundreds of distilleries went under.

Criminality and unrefined liquor undermined the market like a mole beneath a grass lawn.

The prohibition era produced a number of other notorious characters in addition to Remus, for example Capone and the incorruptible Elliot Ness. One well-known gentleman was Captain William McCoy, who shipped Scottish Cutty Sark whisky from the Bahamas to the US coast. He was a quality-conscious supplier who developed a good reputation, so that customers soon wanted nothing but "the real McCoy."

As alcohol consumption escalated so too did criminality, both large and small scale. Bribery and killings were everyday occurrences during the prohibition era. What has been called one of the world's most unsuccessful socio-political experiments ran for 13 years, and lost the American state no less than 11 billion dollars in tax revenue.

In addition to various temporary phenomena and some material for Hollywood, these years also gave rise to some permanent changes. For example, the twenties saw a significant Canadian influence in the North American liquor market; also, as the quality of their liquor was often poor, the Americans developed the habit of mixing their hard liquor. They added angostura, fruit juices, tonic and other things and created new drinks to hide the taints in low-quality liquor; this was a necessity at the time, but can perhaps be seen looking back as a useful contribution to whisky culture.

An end to the misery?

Franklin D Roosevelt came to power promising, amongst other things, to repeal the Prohibition Act. By 1933, the experiment was over and the gangster syndicates had to seek out other areas of activity. The people celebrated, even if there was a fly in the ointment; although the Act was repealed at a federal level

in 1933, Mississippi, the last remaining dry state, didn't revoke the alcohol ban until 1961.

It's worth noting that around three-quarters of Kentucky still has an alcohol ban even today. In these so-called "dry counties," you may not drink alcohol in front of anyone else, nor can you buy alcohol in a shop. In addition to a total ban, certain parts of the US still have legislation which prevents alcohol being seen in public. This is the reason why you often see so-called "brown bagging" in films—Americans sneaking about with their bottle hidden in a brown paper bag.

Ironically, Moore County, where the Jack Daniel Distillery is located, has been a dry county since 1909. And when you hear a Jack Daniel's employee say with a shrug:

"We all go to church and we all drink, but not in front of each other," you could almost be in Sweden.

After the ban had been lifted, the whiskey industry recovered, haltingly. Joy was short-lived, however, as stormclouds gathered over Europe, and after Japan's attack on Pearl Harbor the US was drawn fully into the war. Alcohol was needed for the war, but for purposes very different to intoxication. However this was not entirely a bad thing, since it meant production facilities were kept running and the demands of the war industry prompted improvements in processes and higher quality. When this misery too came to an end, the whiskey industry began to scent new opportunities.

> **"What America needs now is a drink!"**
>
> The famous words of Franklin D Roosevelt on December 5, 1933 when prohibition was repealed.

And what happens next?

The upturn in the US after the war favored this section of the economy too, at least to start with. The passion for US-produced whiskey waned around the 1960s. Distilleries that weren't actually closed were mothballed in anticipation of better times. It wasn't until the 1980s that the Americans began to rediscover their own products. An increasing level of consumption gave rise to ideas for more exclusive products. The more far-sighted producers introduced new developments in the late 1980s such as small-batch and single-barrel whiskey. The fabulous Blanton's Single Barrel turned out to be one of the drivers of this development. It was launched in 1984 and, as the first small-batch whiskey, was in many ways a trendsetter. In the new era that has emerged, with beer production based on micro-breweries and an established wine industry, it now looks as though the native spirit has at long last found its way back to the natives.

In recent years, developments in the US market have been positive. This is especially the case for the more exclusive types of whiskey with more of a hand-crafted profile which have been released in small batches. There is a growing interest in small, niche products for enthusiasts and it looks as though this is increasing the consumption of high-quality whiskey.

This could be threatened by health fanatics working in league with temperance extremists. There is an unspoken worry in the industry that the movement that has for some time been pressurizing the tobacco industry will start to go after the liquor industry, cheered on eagerly by litigation attorneys hungry for commission. Let us hope that this concern does not become a reality. It would be good if the small batches with big aromas could continue to stop us in our tracks and make us realize how great really good American whiskey is.

Well-polished interior at Maker's Mark. (Top) ▲
Nashville streetscene, with celebrities other than Jack D from Tennessee. (Right) ▶

Japan

Five or ten years ago, taking a Japanese whisky to a whisky tasting event would have caused raised eyebrows. If you said "Yoichi" in a bar, you could expect the bartender to reply "Bless you!". Almost everybody associated Asia and whisky with vacation trips to Thailand, when what you'd have in mind would be alcoholic liquor that's best drunk with 7 Up, or not at all.

Today, the situation is quite different. The newly-initiated are fascinated by the quality of Japanese whisky while the established drinkers debate which of the well-matured Japanese whiskies will beat the previous top ranking. The quality is certainly intriguing. The whisky bears all the Japanese hallmarks of well-planned excellence and humble image. These are products which in many respects provoke envy and admiration from their competitors—and delighted smiles from us consumers!

Inspiration from Scotland

Japanese whisky has been greatly inspired by Scotland. This isn't at all surprising, since it was in Scotland that knowledge of whisky production was acquired by the young chemist Masataka Taketsuru. He was sent there by his employer to learn how to set up a distillery and produce whisky. Taketsuru was unquestionably an inquiring, insistent and enthusiastic young man. A visit to Speyside in spring 1919 was followed by studies in chemistry in Glasgow and then a traineeship. The distilleries Taketsuru visited included Longmorn in Speyside, the now closed Bo'ness column-still distillery in Linlithgow, and Hazelburn in Campbeltown, the latter also closed down but surviving as a brand in the Springbank range. Taketsuru documented his traineeship in minute detail, keeping records and writing notes in the margins of his textbooks. In this way, and through good mentoring at the distilleries, the foundations were laid for the knowledge that during the coming decade was to become the seedbed for the Japanese whisky industry. As if in a poem by Burns,

◀ *View over the Hakusha distillery in spring. In the picture above, the same distillery's pagodas extending above the treetops.*

Taketsuru also found love amongst the lanes and distilleries of Campbeltown, and he married before he returned to Japan. By autumn 1920 he was back in Japan, full of inspiration and, we must assume, floating on the fluffy little clouds of love—in his case, with a slight aroma of peat-smoke.

However, Taketsuru had a hard uphill climb ahead of him before he could put into practice what he had learned in Scotland. His employer at the time of leaving for Scotland, Kihei Abe at Settsu, a liquor company making essences and fake liquor, had abandoned plans to make real whisky due to the poor economic climate after the First World War. Taketsuru therefore resigned from the company and was recruited shortly afterwards by Shinjiro Torii. Torii had made money selling wine and wine imitations through his company Kotobukiya. So, together with Torii, Taketsuru built up Japan's first whisky distillery in the small town of Yamazaki. The company was renamed as the now more familiar Suntory, the second part being based on Torii's name. The first product had a very pronounced peat-smoke character, and the launch in 1929 was something of a fiasco. As a result of this, Taketsuru stepped away from whisky production at Suntory. He left the company in 1934 and started Nikka in the same year, in competition with his previous partner. Suntory continued down the same path, although they toned down the smokiness of their subsequent whiskies. Nikka's first steps were faltering ones. The distillery experienced several years of economic hardship before it was taken under the wing of the Imperial Navy and didn't find its feet until the outbreak of the Second World War.

Interestingly in this context, the Yamazaki distillery is usually said to be the first Japanese whisky distillery, but the small White Oak Distillery in Akashi got a license for whisky production the same year Taketsuru traveled to Scotland—even though the stills had not at that time been installed!

For small and large distilleries alike it was, however, the domestic market that was to be by far the dominant one for several decades. The two great pioneering companies Suntory and Nikka continue to dominate to this day, having 80–90% of the market. There are about ten distilleries supplying the whisky and soda-drinking Japanese with the basic liquor for the highballs they take in at every opportunity. The 1990s saw a significant change in behavior both amongst the Japanese and in the Japanese whisky industry, when there was a decline in the popularity of blended whisky. The Japanese whisky industry took the opportunity then to promote malt whisky. Exports also got underway around this time, although the overseas market even today is small in comparison with the volumes produced for the enormous domestic market.

"...of all the peated whiskies of the world, only Ardbeg can stand shoulder to shoulder with Yoichi when it comes to sheer complexity."

Jim Murray's Whisky Bible

◀ *Visual inspection of liquor at Yamazaki's current distillery, and, to the right, the exterior of the old one.*

International awards and media attention follow when Japanese whisky ventures into international markets. Japan is acclaimed in *Whisky Magazine* and *Malt Advocate* as well as by commentators such as Jim Murray in his *Whisky Bible*, with the result that more and more people want to experience the Japanese marvel. Yamazaki is climbing up towards the highest position in the top-ten list of the world's best-selling malt whiskies. Names such as Yamazaki, Hakushu, Karuizawa and Yoichi are now renowned throughout the world for their quality, and hence also known in the barren regions on the other side of the world where Masataka Taketsuru learned how to make malt whisky just under a hundred years ago.

Several distilleries in one

The Scottish influence on Japanese whisky is apparent in terms of raw materials, the design of production processes and the finished result. The malt is often bought from Scotland, and the stills and equipment are similar. However, one crucial difference between Scotland and Japan is the trading in casks between distilleries and blenders, something that in practice rarely happens with distillery companies in Japan. One major reason for this is the early rivalry between the founders of Suntory and Nikka. Consequently, each company has had to become self-sufficient for historical reasons and has had to create its palette of whisky with different flavors and aromas by itself.

Despite continuing to engage in polite trench warfare, however, the Japanese have had more success with blending. They vary the character of the whisky within the same distillery firstly by varying the extent to which the malt is smoked. Variety is also achieved by using several strains of yeast that contribute different flavors. Likewise, producers use different-sized fermenting vessels and also fermentation in varying degrees, where short or long fermentation times give grassy, creamy or fruity qualities to the end product. Another important factor is the combination of stills of different shape. An example of this is Yamazaki's six wash stills and six liquor stills. These vary in size and design, which provides a great deal of scope to change the character of the distillate. Another new and rather unusual way to flavor the liquor before maturing is to filter the distillate through bamboo charcoal. This is obviously a step inspired by the so-called Lincoln County process, in which Jack Daniel's and the neighboring Dickel's distillery in Tennessee filter their raw liquor through maple charcoal before it is put into the cask. It smooths away the sharpest tones in the liquor before it is put into casks for maturation.

Finally, a whole range of different aromas and flavors are achieved by using different types of cask. It is mostly American casks that are used. Up to 90% of the raw liquor that is produced is put into bourbon casks or casks from Jack Daniel's. The remaining 10% of casks are mainly sherry casks but a small number of Japanese oak (mizunara) casks are also used. This gives the whisky more of a tannin flavor, sandalwood tones and also sweetness. Japanese oak is used only sparingly as it is in limited supply.

There is also some experimenting, for example at Yamazaki, with casks that have contained plum liqueur and also with casks of cedar or oak casks with sandalwood elements.

Japanese oak, *Quercus mongolica*

Mizunara, also called Japanese water oak, grows in eastern Asia but is increasingly rare in Japan. The largest stands have been on Hokkaido, but felling has drastically reduced availability. This tree is also said to have paid a high price as material for coffins during the First World War. It is more difficult to make functional, water-tight casks from the relatively soft wood of the water oak than from American or European oak. Use of water oak as material for maturation casks therefore declined when American oak casks came onto the Japanese market after the Second World War.

The effect the water oak has on whisky is noticeable in some older Yamazaki bottlings, and of course in bottlings where it is obvious that water oak, or mizunara, has been used for maturation. The character this oak gives to the whisky is sandalwood, cedar and something approaching smoke-like wood tones; some have identified the latter as aloe wood, mentioned in the Bible as having a sweet smell, like myrrh, when placed on glowing coals. Water oak sometimes also gives a touch of ripe fruit, such as coconut, and also terpenes such as camphor, mint and old leaves. Unusual, with a suggestion of reverence, and perhaps therefore typically Japanese?

Other whisky-producing countries

Amateurs who turn pro

Most of us are content simply to enjoy a whisky when we feel in the mood. Some of us go to tastings to find out a bit more about the history and background of our favorite whisky. A few more may arrange tastings, and may have been on a course about whisky and spent a week or two in overalls at a distillery, so as to learn in detail how whisky is produced; to make ourselves at home in the distillery, have our noses filled with the aromas of mashing, breathe in the earthy tone of damp warehouses and experience the pungent, warm aromas from a smoking kiln. As if this were not enough, there are also those absolute fanatics who go that extra mile. This includes those who have started up magazines, who organize fairs and who write books. Nevertheless—we are all observers.

In addition to all those mentioned, there is the group that has taken its interest to an even higher level: those who have become producers—professionals, laymen and devoted amateurs who have taken the step over to the other side. Many of them have sprung from the fertile topsoil from which countless small breweries sprout and grow strong, sustained simply by their enthusiasm and an irrepressible desire to achieve the perfect beer or the purest fruity distillate. We're talking about those who have turned pro. This small set of people enlarges the pool of authorities we can all interrogate, visit or listen to. A few paragraphs follow about these enthusiasts of all kinds all around the world: those challenging and complementing the countries and producers that are already established.

England and Wales

Historically, whisky has, of course, also been produced within the United Kingdom outside Ireland and Scotland. The Irish were also close to biting the dust, the fate suffered by the English, at one point. However, both the English and Welsh made comebacks a few years ago, at St George's Distillery in Norfolk in 2006, and Penderyn in 1998. There are about a dozen varieties of St George, both clearly fruity and heavily smoky. Penderyn is a full-bodied, fruit-flavored candy creation with elements of white mould cheese, one of the characteristics that can sometimes be found in certain rums.

Germany

With their many itinerant fruit distilleries and many fruity distillates it was probably only a matter of time before the Germans started distilling grain liquor and maturing it in oak casks. In addition, they have, as expected, taken advantage of local opportunities for storage in wine casks. Of the just under ten producers, Slyrs is worth a mention; they have established an export business to other European countries and also to the US and Australia. Another big shot is Blaue Maus, which, with its tannic oak style and young spirit, almost reminiscent of malt grappa, has, since its early launch in 1986 (as Glen Mouse!), now acquired siblings in the family, including Spinnaker, Grüne Hund and Schwarzer Pirat.

Liechtenstein

Any self-respecting principality should obviously have a whisky distillery. And this is the case with Liechtenstein, where the producer, Telser, has been producing malt distillates, and also fruit distillate and vodka, since 2006. In addition to its broad range, its production is characterized by limited editions and experimental product development. A curiosity worth mentioning is that this distillery is rather unique in using firewood to heat its stills.

France

Despite the greatest possible competition from cognac, armagnac and calvados, a couple of whisky producers have nevertheless managed to gain a foothold in France. This ought to be the case, since more whisky is actually drunk than cognac in this country. The whisky comes from Distillerie Bertrand in the historical beer-making province of Alsace and from Brittany with its Gaelic heritage,

where Glann ar Mor and Warenghem are located. The latter has its malt, Armorik, and the blend, Breton, and Glann ar Mor produces an unsmoked whisky of the same name and nowadays also the smoky Kornog. In addition to these distilleries, Distillerie Guillon in Champagne is worth mentioning in particular for its many whisky varieties matured in wine casks.

Belgium

The Belgians have of course a good reputation for their beer production and they are world class when it comes to quantity, quality and also tradition. Nowadays, they also produce stronger products, for example under the names The Belgian Owl and Het Anker. The latter is better known in the beer world; it dates back to 1369 although it has only been producing whisky since 2003.

Holland

The Dutch also go back a long way in terms of their beer traditions, but they are beginners when it comes to whisky. The former gin distillery, Zuidam, has been working away since 1998 and this seniority has now attracted the attention of, among others, *Whisky Magazine*. In addition to Zuidam, there are currently two further producers, Us Heit and Vallei.

The Czech Republic

Scandals relating to hard liquor have hit this beer paradise of late. Beer distillates are available to purchase but, in terms of both purity and whisky character, they leave a great deal to be desired. Gold Cock whisky was founded as early as 1877 but went under and was bought up by the slivovitz producer Rudolf Jelinek, who has now started Gold Cock up again and done so with distinction. It is also worth mentioning that those who hunt around in liquor delicatessens may, if they're lucky, find the unusual Hammer Head, which was produced up to the 1990s and then fell with a thud like the Berlin Wall.

Austria

Have you seen or even sampled Austrian whisky in its expensive square bottles already? It has a lot of spirity youthfulness and is not always a polished act, but is nonetheless full of character. Of the five distilleries currently in existence in Austria, it is worth mentioning the distilling breweries Roggenhof, which was first in the country to distil whisky, and Rabenbräu, with its Old Raven whisky. Both of these produce exclusive, limited edition whiskies. Another entrepreneur in this area is Hans Riesetbauer, who, as well as having established himself as a producer of fruit distillates, has also been producing malt whisky since 1995. The latter is matured in the manner dictated by conditions in the country: in used chardonnay and dessert wine casks.

Switzerland

In the town of Elfingen in Aargau lies Whisky Castle and the distillery run by the Käser family, where one of the distillery's products is produced only by the light of the full moon. With Transylvanian influences, one might imagine. They also have a number of other products with varying strengths and types of cask. As an observant liquor purchaser you may already have seen Swiss whisky—but it has only been available on the shelves since the turn of the century. This is because, from the First World War until July 1, 1999, it was forbidden to produce distillates from foodstuffs such as grain and potatoes. Amongst the others who took the opportunity to begin whisky distillation at that time were the producers Zürcher, Locher, Hollen, and Hagen. As in Austria, production is in relatively small volumes and the producers are keen to experiment, for example using different types of wine cask.

Finland

The Finnish malt whisky, Teerenpeli, has its origins in a small chain with a couple of pub breweries in Finland. In Lahti, the chain bought pot stills in 2002 and that is what they continue to use. The whisky has been launched and is a promising, young product, with faithful customers in the chain's restaurants. The whisky has fitted in well there with Teerenpeli's overall concept of food and drink and the whisky has also attracted attention outside restaurants and even outside Finland.

Denmark

The Danes have an ancient beer tradition and have also had a rapidly-growing culture of microbreweries for some years. A couple of the breweries, with the Copenhagen-based Braunstein at the forefront, have begun to distil their malt brews. The excellent outcome of this activity is a number of exclusive products that bear similarities both to young Scottish whiskies

and, for that matter, also to products from neighboring countries. Other producers in Denmark at this stage are Stauning Whisky, Ørbæk Bryggeri, and Fary Lochan Destilleri.

Sweden

With its core of devoted whisky enthusiasts, the Swedes have now crossed the threshold and begun to produce whisky with a vengeance. There are a dozen players. On average, the world's whisky drinkers consume about ten percent malt whisky as a proportion of total whisky purchases. In Sweden, the figure is about twenty percent, which is the highest in the world. This means there is a good basis for demand for the current initiatives in Swedish whisky production. Mackmyra started the process as early as 1999 and has now been followed by others including Spirit of Hven, Box, Smögen Whisky, Wannborga, Norrtelje Brenneri, and Gammelstilla. And there is a lot more going on in the fertile Swedish whisky environment.

There are many others awaiting the three-year maturation point or who have just begun producing raw whisky, for example Bergslagen, Gotland Whisky, Grythyttan, and Arvidsjaur.

Spain

Somewhat unexpectedly, Spain's only whisky distillery is neither new nor small. Established in 1959 and in production in 1962, with an annual capacity of more than two million gallons (eight million liters) it is a medium-sized player. Blended whisky is produced here under the name of "DYC," as well as a blended malt with Scottish ingredients.

Russia

Wine products and also whisky have been produced at the Kizlyarskoye distillery in the republic of Dagestan in Russia since 1948. Whisky production has been sporadic and the stills have been used mainly for brandy. We are, however, watching with anticipation to see how things develop, as there is a daily capacity here of 800 gallons (around 3,000 liters) from the plant's four pot stills.

Canada

The other big country in the west has a distillery tradition as old as that of the US. The Canadians have, however, mainly stuck to blends in enormous volumes, sometimes with a splash of fruit juice to enhance the taste and usually bearing great similarities to simple bourbons. Since around the turn of the century, however, the Canadians too have moved towards micro-distilleries. With distilleries such as Kittling Ridge, founded in 1992 in Ontario, and also the malt whisky distillery Glenora in Nova Scotia, Canada can now boast of more than just quantity. And, of course, a distillery in Nova Scotia is a must, particularly since jealous lawyers for the Scotch Whisky Association have been muttering about the cheek of being located in a place with such a Scottish ring to it and also producing malt whisky. Ouch! Their Glen Breton whisky is available in both traditional casks and also matured in an ice wine barrel!

Australia

Obviously the old penal colony has a great gene pool of involuntarily emigrated Scots and Irish. Despite this, only a couple of distilleries have flourished, including in Tasmania. At best, good malt whisky and, if nothing else, interesting products.

India

More than a billion people and a British heritage, so what do you expect? Recently, a list was produced of the ten best-selling whiskies from around the world, in terms of volume. Seven were Indian. Any questions? Yes, one perhaps: where did the other three come from? The answer is the Scottish whiskies Johnnie Walker and Ballantine's, and the American Jack Daniel's.

Well-known, certainly, but perhaps Officer's Choice, Bagpiper's and McDowell's are names you should commit to memory now that India's interest in whisky has been awoken with a start. In terms of malts, I would also mention the often sensationally well-matured Amrut from Bangalore. Just as in the West Indies and Kentucky, high temperatures contribute to accelerated maturation in the cask. Amrut is available in everything from light, spirity, peat-smoke tastes to unique, sherry-fruity, matured products with characteristics that should be cause for concern at a Scottish castle or two.

Taiwan

The multi-prizewinning Kavalan has put a young whisky nation on the map with a vengeance. The founders are said to have received many different suggestions of whisky types to produce but maintained that it was Scottish whisky they wished to imitate. Like the Japanese they pulled this off very well. Here, the conditions for production and the maturation climate make for a sensational whisky with a rich sweetness. Here's to more of the same!

South Africa

With a well-established wine industry, it also makes fortified wines and brandy. As a result of its British heritage, whisky has been produced for about a century and was already being drunk when Churchill was putting a splash of water into his whisky to clean the water. In 1977, James Sedgewick started up the successful malt whisky brand, Three Ships, with both malt and corn distillate, which has also paved the way for other producers.

Since 1948

AMRUT
100

PEATED SINGLE MALT
WHISKY

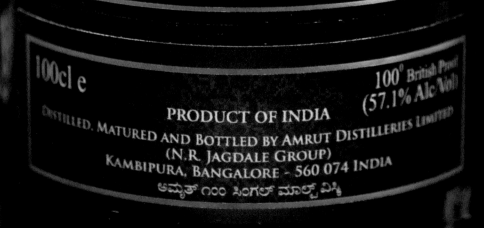

100cl e

100° British Proof
(57.1% Alc/Vol)

PRODUCT OF INDIA

DISTILLED, MATURED AND BOTTLED BY AMRUT DISTILLERIES LIMITED
(N.R. JAGDALE GROUP)
KAMBIPURA, BANGALORE - 560 074 INDIA

ಅಮೃತ್ ೧೦೦ ಸಿಂಗಲ್ ಮಾಲ್ಟ್ ವಿಸ್ಕಿ

Whisky production

Any self-respecting book about whisky contains a section about production. If you are one of the anorak-wearing types at home with a camera and notebook observing mashing and accustomed to making your way among the casks in the storage warehouses, then you can probably skim quickly through this chapter. If, on the other hand, you belong to the happy flock that has just acquired a taste for whisky, have visited your first distillery or only want to find out more about how whisky is made, then you have an interesting chapter containing basic facts about whisky ahead of you. There is a thorough analysis of malt whisky, but also some space devoted to corn and unmalted barley. The magnifying glass is particularly focused on what it is that provides the taste since this is the most important thing for us, is it not?

From barley to whisky

The barley

There are a couple of answers, both just as sensible, to the question of why barley began to be used for whisky in the first place. One of these is the obvious one: barley was used because that was what was available. Beer had been made from barley throughout living memory. When returning monks and men with a medical education taught others the art of distilling, it was, however, the alcoholic fermented raw material that was readily available that was initially used, i.e., wine. But soon enough, perhaps as early as the 12th century, a mash using only barley began to be used. In other words, they began to distil beer instead of wine.

Another reason why barley is still used today, when other kinds of grain are actually available, is that barley is one of God's best whisky raw product packages—compared with other types of grain, barley has a high starch content, which can be converted into fermentable sugar. Also, and rather practically, barley contains the tool to break down the starch, i.e., the necessary enzymes.

◀ *One of the stills in Mackmyra's gravitational distillery.*

The character of the barley is managed during cultivation so that the starch content is kept as high as possible and the protein content kept low. This is achieved through limited use of fertilizers. It's the starch that is most desirable if there is to be success at the first stage of whisky production, when producers want to achieve the maximum volume of alcohol in relation to the amount of barley used. The grain is an expensive raw material, regardless of the kind of whisky produced, and this influences what is expected from its properties.

Other properties that the barley requires relate to the properties of the final whisky. For this reason, development work is constantly ongoing within the grain industry with new kinds of barley being produced in development cycles of just over ten years. An old classic that is often much appreciated for its properties is Golden Promise. A number of other, newer types of barley are used, including Optic, Prisma, Chariot, and Derkado. The barley certainly has a distinct impact on the alcohol yield during production; however, the impact of the barley on the character of the final product is not as clear. The difference in the taste and aroma of a whisky as a result of the choice of type of barley is negligible.

As we know, it is not just barley that is used. Rye, corn and wheat have been used in the US and Canada purely for climate-related reasons; it was what was available there when the countries were established. The disadvantage with the crops that grow best in the warmer climate of these countries is that they contain lower percentages of the enzymes that break down the starch into fermentable sugar. For this reason, some barley malt is also used in, for example, bourbon. The percentage of barley malt in a raw product recipe, a so-called mash bill, is typically around 15% for a bourbon. In addition, the mix of the other raw products in a bourbon is subject to legal requirements in America and also preferences regarding taste. By law, a bourbon must contain at least 51% corn, a rye whiskey a corresponding amount of rye, wheat

whiskey 51% wheat and a malt whiskey at least 51% barley malt. However, a bourbon will normally typically contain about 70% corn and 15% barley, while the remainder is often rye, although a few producers have replaced this with wheat to give the liquor a somewhat lighter and less harsh character.

Steeping and germination

The introductory stages of both whisky and whiskey production involve mashing. In brief, this involves processing the raw product so that it can be converted into a wash with a low alcoholic content, which can, in turn, be distilled to increase its strength and then matured in oak casks. This is roughly the procedure regardless of which type of liquor is being produced. Whether liquor is being made from potatoes, wheat or rice, the starch must be broken down into fermentable sugar. In the case of industrial column distilleries, this is done through pressure cooking but the description below focuses on the basic elements of traditional malt whisky production which takes place in so-called pot stills.

It is also worth mentioning here that most malt is now produced in large-scale malthouses that act as subcontractors and are separate from the distilleries. This is where all the introductory stages take place, from the barley being delivered from the farmer to steeping, germinating, kilning and then delivery to the distilleries. The process uses methods that are different in their design from manual procedures, although the goal is the same. The malthouses employ mechanical solutions, while the craftsman uses manpower. The malthouses produce their malt according to strictly controlled processes, with very high and consistent quality levels and fully in accordance with requirements for peaty character or anything else specified by the individual distillery.

For our basic knowledge of whisky, we return, however, to how things were done in the past and continue to be done today at a handful of Scotland's malt whisky distilleries. There, the first step in

transforming the barley into a malt whisky involves tricking the barley into thinking it's springtime. This is done by thoroughly soaking the barley in a process known as steeping. Once the barley has been steeped a couple of times, it is spread out on what is known as a malting floor where it is allowed to germinate for a couple of weeks, and tended regularly.

The purpose of germination is to release the barley's riches—the starch and enzymes—so that they can begin the conversion of the starch into sugar in future stages of the process. What happens when the germ begin to sprout in the barley is that the cell walls of the barley burst. This makes the starch and enzymes more accessible to each other than is the case with unmalted barley. The germinating barley, called green malt, is tended to by being turned regularly during germination. This is done by circulating the green malt using something resembling an electric rotavator to ensure ventilation and to keep the temperature down. Heat is produced during germination and needs to be ventilated away for two reasons: the enzymes are temperature-sensitive, and best results are achieved if the temperature can be kept just below 68 degrees (about 20°C) during germination.

Once the barley has sprouted a sixteenth of an inch (a couple of millimeters) or so, the next step begins. This involves brutally killing the germinating barley. The reason for this is that the germ does as nature intends and uses the starch in the barley as energy when it grows. So the more the germ grows, the less is left over for liquor production. In other words, there is a balancing act between allowing the green malt to reach the stage where the cell walls are sufficiently broken down but, at the same time, avoiding any unnecessary consumption of the valuable starch.

Kilning

Heat is used to kill the germ and end germination. The barley is roasted in a process known to beer or whisky producers as kilning. Originally, the green malt was put in a heated room with an open fire. Nowadays, warm air is circulated through the moist green malt so that it dries. Kilning takes place in the part of the distillery that is perhaps most conspicuous, i.e., the kiln. In many of the distilleries that first saw the light of day in the late 19th century, the kiln is the pagoda-like building that rises up wherever whisky is produced in Scotland: the building that has become as much a symbol of whisky production as the copper still itself. The architect behind it was Charles Cree Doig (1855–1918) and this pagoda, sometimes also called the Doig Ventilator, was built for the first time as a commission at the Daluanie distillery in Dufftown in Scotland.

From the bottom upwards, the kiln is a furnace at the bottom of a chimney with a fair-sized waist, like a funnel on a funnel. The space is divided in two by a floor made of a fine-meshed metal net. The germinating green malt is spread out on this floor so that hot air and smoke from the furnace can flow through it. The kiln narrows off towards the top and the structure has its elegant finale in the chimney that is topped off on the outside with a small roof.

The fuel chosen for the kiln determines whether or not the whisky will taste of peat-smoke. Peat was originally used as fuel for the same reason that barley became the raw material—peat was the fuel available. Increasing industrialization and better transportation provided whisky producers with the opportunity to increase their margins, however, since they could now buy in fuels that were more effective than peat, which produced more smoke than fire and heat. This crass financial argument meant the smoky character of some producers' whiskies disappeared as peat was phased out. The effect of this can still be seen today. A peat-smoke taste is primarily still to be found in the products of the peripheral distilleries that historically suffered from the fact that coal and coke required lengthy transportation. Their costs for fuel other than local peat were higher. The conclusion of this, of course, is that we might by now have expected economics to have led to non-smoked whisky everywhere. In order to preserve their heritage, however, a number of producers continue to use peat as fuel for kilning, which is pleasing for those of us who enjoy the marine, smoky tone of Islay whisky or Highland Park's peaty background tones.

As previously mentioned, the primary purpose of kilning is to stop germination. Another positive outcome of roasting is that dried malt has a much longer shelf-life than unprocessed barley; also, kilning can add to the taste of the whisky by using peat, which also improves shelf-life as a result of the disinfectant effect of the phenols. The amount of phenols from the smoke that is caught on the outside of and within the malt is usually measured in parts per million, ppm, of phenols. Traditionally, it has always been the phenol content of the malt that has been under discussion, probably because it is in the malt that producers have specified the smokiness of a whisky mash bill. This may, however, appear strange to us as consumers. It's like asking the chef how many pounds of black pepper he has in the pantry instead of tasting the pepper sauce he's made. This has, however, begun to change. There is more frequent reference to the ppm of phenols in the final raw liquor, which seems much more relevant. About a third of the phenol content referred to in the malt remains in the whisky. A specific example is Lagavulin, which, according to Graham Logie who was distillery manager between the years of 2006 and 2008, starts at 30–40 ppm in the malt and ends up with about 10–15 ppm of phenols in the liquor. In addition to this, Logie revealed the thought-provoking fact that the same malt recipe is used for Caol Ila, Lagavulin, and Laphroaig, i.e., the same phenol content, and the same type of yeast is also used. In other words, the differences are in how the mashing and distillation are carried out and also the design of the still, as well as how they are matured and finally blended before being bottled.

◀ *Hard work achieving a good smoky malt at Glenfiddich. (Top)*
◀ *Peat-digging on Islay. (Bottom left)*
◀ *Peat supply at the kiln outside Mackmyra's gravitational distillery. (Bottom right)*

Not just the cask that provides taste

After kilning, the next stages involve making use of the valuable properties of the malt. More interesting than the tricks of the trade is how those properties affect the taste of the whisky in your glass. This is particularly the case because the Scottish malt whisky produced today is still primarily used as an ingredient in blended whisky, as a flavoring you could say. About ninety percent of all whisky sold throughout the world is blended whisky, although only about 80% in my malt-loving homeland of Sweden. From this point of view, the most important thing about malt whisky is that it has a clear and consistent character. We talk of properties such as smokiness, sweetness, fruitiness, oiliness and grassiness. You also experience this type of basic characteristic when you yourself smell a whisky during a tasting or sitting at home on the sofa. A much more difficult part of the jigsaw is finding characteristics that match. Two different types of malt whisky with a sweet taste can have a completely different effect as part of a blend, depending on their other characteristic traits of oiliness, malt taste, smokiness and so forth. This explains why, to get a good blend, it is so important to choose a base, the grain liquor, that combines well with the other ingredients.

The character of a whisky emerges during maturation, however. Broadly speaking, about two thirds of the color, aroma and whisky character come from maturation in the cask. Mashing, fermentation and distillation certainly have a considerable effect on the aroma, flavor and mouthfeel of the raw liquor and thereby also the whisky. The effect they have can be managed with precision nowadays, which is largely the result of research into the factors that give rise to the various qualities of the end product. I say nowadays because many of the contributory chemical and biological reactions were not known just a few decades ago. This was a time when the distilleries would beat their chests and proudly declare how they made the best whisky in the world. Surprisingly enough, they were rather taken aback if you dared to ask what it was that made it so good.

◀ *The extremely cultivated Henric Molin among the fermenting tubs at Spirit of Hven. (Top)*
◀ *Stills at Ardbeg. (Bottom, right)*

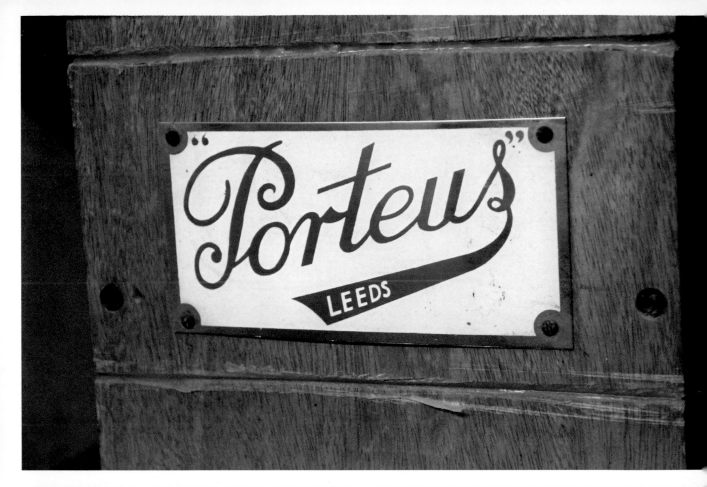

Grinding and mashing

The malt is ground and then the mashing process follows. As a result of these operations the raw product's assets are exposed and extracted for the world to enjoy. The malt is ground into fine particles and then leached with hot water. Grinding is important, not just for making everything possible, but also for the flavor. This is because a more finely-ground mix in the grist, with more finer flour and less coarse flour (grits) and husks, determines the results of mashing.

Fine flour means more sugar can be released from the malt's starch, which leads, therefore, to more alcohol. More fine flour in the grist also gives a greater yield of the substances that give the wort and also the liquor an oilier character. The composition of the grist is determined by the grinding and a normal level of fine flour is around ten or so percent, but experiments have been performed at, for example, the Teaninich distillery involving grinding using hammer mills and this gives a very high percentage of fine flour. In addition, they skip the traditional mash tun there. Instead they use a combined process where the grist and hot water are first mixed in a tank. The conversion from starch to fermentable sugar takes place in this container with the help of the enzymes contained in the barley. The liquid that is then pumped out at this stage is filtered more carefully than is normally the case. This is done using pressure, using a filter that separates out the coarser particles in the wort to a greater extent than a strainer in a normal mash tun is capable of. The result of this is a wort containing fewer solid particles and more of the components that lend an oiliness to the final result.

▲ *Demonstration of the levels of grinding at Glenfarclas. Note the content of the scoop, with husks and coarse flour and fine flour: grits, grist, flour.*
◀ *A study of mills: at bottom left the new mill at Mackmyra's gravitational distillery.*

Fermentation

Most of the character of the raw liquor is produced during fermentation. Everyone in the brewing industry knows that the yeast affects the character of the final result. There the way the yeast is looked after is reminiscent of how sacred cows are handled in India—carefully, cautiously and with dignity. In the whisky industry, it has been primarily American producers who have historically considered yeast highly important for taste. This trend can now be seen in other whisky-producing countries. In the US, their attention to the care and choice of yeast manifests itself in, among other things, their own highly-valued yeasts being stored like the family jewels in several different geographical locations, so that they can survive power cuts and other catastrophes without individual strains dying out or degenerating.

Nowadays, a Scotsman also chooses his yeast carefully when it comes to producing whisky. The length of fermentation affects the growth of bacteria. A rapid fermentation reduces the chances of bacteria growing and thereby reduces the element of acidity in the wash that the bacteria contribute to. In terms of flavor, the effect of this is that the raw liquor becomes fruitier with a greater degree of acidity in the wash. This is because the reactions of the acids with the copper stills during distillation add a fruitiness to the raw liquor. A producer desiring a sharper, grassier tone in his whisky will thereby choose a hard-working yeast that consumes the sugar in the wash quickly. Those desiring a more acidic wash instead, and a fruitier whisky with more esters, will choose a yeast that chews through the sugar content of the mash at a somewhat slower tempo. But how long actually is long? This obviously varies depending on the conditions, but after about 40 hours no further alcohol is produced. If fermentation is allowed to continue for twice as long, 80 hours, the otherwise grassy character will clearly have developed into a more acidic, in other words fruitier, whisky. Often the fermentation time at distilleries varies because it is allowed to continue for longer on weekends. In terms of extremes, a first example in this context would be Tomatin, where fermentation is quick and lasts only 46–48 hours. On the other hand, there are producers like Cardhu with long fermentation periods, averaging 65 hours, or Glenfiddich, where, with fermentation lasting between 55 and 72 hours, there are fermentation buildings where there is already a heavy, sweet and fruity aroma in parts of the distillery at the fermentation stage.

Distillation

As we know, each stage of the distillation process gives the raw liquor increasing purity. Other ways to determine the flavor of the raw liquor and which substances accompany it from the still are temperature and time. This is largely governed by how the distiller decides to make his cut. Put simply, the cut decides how little or how much of what comes out of the still is collected. It's done by controlling when to start collecting what is coming from the still and when to stop. Calculated on the basis of percentage of alcohol per volume, the first drops collected will have a high alcoholic content; once the distillation has been depleted of its ethanol, after a few hours, this will reduce and the receiver will on the other hand become increasingly full.

The three main elements of distillation are usually called head, heart and tail. In other words, it is how big a heart the producer decides to collect that governs a great deal of the flavor of the raw liquor. The temperature rises as a result of distillation. If the distiller decides to allow the beginning of the heart to touch on the head, the liquor will have a more flowery and lighter character. If the heart acquires part of the tail, the raw liquor will be oilier and heavier and, if the prerequisites are there from the malt, also smokier.

The reason this happens is that the components in the wash that are light in chemical terms, the substances with a low boiling point, evaporate away early when

the temperature is somewhat lower. These substances give the liquor a fruity, flowery characteristic. The middle section contains purer ethanol. Heavier substances, with a higher boiling point, then follow in the tail. These are also able to float away at this point, as the temperature gradually rises to such an extent that these too acquire the energy to evaporate.

Cut-off points for some distilleries

How the heart is cut determines to a great extent how flowery, fruity, sharp, rich, smoky or oily a raw liquor becomes. You can see below some random samples of ethanol levels at the first and second cut-off points. The cut-off points indicate the percentage of ethanol, which is higher at the beginning and lower once the heart is cut on the way in to the tail. The strength at the cut-off points gives an idea of how the distiller is thinking, for example, when, during the second cut-off point, Inchgower or Lagavulin slide over to the heavier alcohols at the start of the tail and allow the ethanol level to fall down towards 55%. This gives a considerable amount of smoky flavoring and an oily and rich character to the raw liquor, while an earlier second cut produces a lighter raw liquor.

The point at which the collecting of the heart of the

Cleaning the stills after production at the distillery at Mackmyra Bruk.

distillation starts and stops is most easily calculated in percentage alcohol by volume. Starting at 80–78% gives a clear fruitiness. Down towards 75%, the character becomes more grassy and vegetal rather than fruity.

Auchentoshan, second cut-off point 81% (triple distilled, perfumey and fruity)

Ardbeg 75–62% (late end to utilize phenols)

Cardhu 80–65% (soft, fruity)

Clynelish 78–60% (fruity)

Glen Moray 74–64% (soft, fruity)

Glen Ord 75–60% (grassy)

Glenfarclas 74–59% (oily, fruity)

Glengoyne 74–63% (soft, fruity)

Glenmorangie 74–60% (fruity, light)

Inchgower, second cut-off point 55% (oily)

Lagavulin, second cut-off point 53% (very long tail to collect phenols and oiliness)

Laphroaig, second cut-off point 61% (late end, also to utilize phenols)

Mackmyra elegant, approx. 74–63% (fruity, light, exact level determined though aroma assessment)

Springbank 75–63% (full-bodied, fruity, aromatic)

Teaninich 72–63% (oily, vegetal)

(This information has been obtained from the distilleries and may vary somewhat over time.)

BRUICHLADDICH
PROGRESSIVE HEBRIDEAN
DISTILLERS
Spirit
AGE 2003 STR
Rotation 12 D14 Size
Cask No 302
Date Drawn 30.3.11
Drawn By
Duty Paid Sample

5336
479
5334
497 1999
J.&G. GRANT
1999

2077 1991
496
BOWMORE DISTILLERY
ISLAY
2067 1997
466

Starting at 72% means the liquor will be perceived as more oily, since the vegetal tones will have abated and been allowed to run down into the slops along with the rest of the head. These slops will be redistilled, it is true, but they will not be matured and later bottled. A distiller who allows the heart to develop at a higher temperature and with a lower ethanol content but more heavy alcohols, will again get a grassiness that is now oily at between 63–60% and, below this, down to 55%, will also obtain raw liquor with both a more full-bodied, fruitier mouthfeel and also phenols, in the form of a smokiness that is probably welcome. In the worst case scenario this will involve an increasing risk of also collecting distillate with undesirable sulfurous tones, for example of gunpowder, rubber or perhaps on the fleshy side.

Other influences

Sulfurous tones in the liquor can also be kept at a low level by maintaining a somewhat higher distillation temperature. The same applies during cooling, which happens more slowly if it takes place at a higher temperature and then allows a great deal of contact between copper and raw liquor. Contact with the copper reduces sulfurous components throughout the entire process, regardless of whether this happens during cooling or earlier, for example, as a result of a copious reflux in the distillation stills.

Finally, it's worth noting that a whisky's mouthfeel may also derive from other technical production properties. An example of this is the waxy feel of Clynelish, which is due to the fact that the result of the first distillation—the low wines—and the distillation remains from the second distillation—the head and the tail—respectively are kept in separate tanks prior to the second distillation. They are usually mixed directly in a vessel which results in a mouthfeel with a less waxy character.

Maturation

As previously mentioned, maturation is the stage that is perhaps most important when it comes to how the whisky will finally smell and taste. During maturation, three principal things happen to the whisky: substances are added to the liquor; substances disappear from the liquor; and there is an interaction between the liquor and the cask.

The characteristics arising from maturation in casks depend on the type of oak in the cask, what has been in the cask before the whisky, how many times the cask has been used, how hard the cask is toasted or charred on the inside, the strength of the liquor and the size of the cask.

In the case of Scotland and also other parts of the world, used bourbon or Tennessee whiskey casks are most common, with around 95% percent of today's whiskies being put into American casks. The remaining 5% of whiskies in Scotland are in sherry casks and there is occasional use of port, Madeira or other kinds of cask. The American white oak gives strong elements of vanilla and resin and also distinct oak tones, as well as so-called lactones. These casks also provide some characteristics of bourbon of course. Sherry (usually oloroso) casks, on the other hand, give you what you would expect from a sherry, i.e., nutty and grapey tones with a touch of chocolate, like raisins or other dried fruit. The fact that sherry casks are usually made from European oak also means that these casks give off more color.

> "Until a man has the luck to chance on a perfectly matured malt, he does not really know what whisky is."
>
> Neil M Gunn (1891–1973),
> a customs and excise official and author.

As well as having previously contained sherry or bourbon, the cask may also have contained whisky for a number of years. This naturally leaches out of the cask but this may also be an advantage if the intention is to mature whisky for a long time. In that case, only a small contribution to the whisky is required each year. Otherwise, things will go too far and the raw liquor's house character may disappear into a swamp of excessively fruity aromas.

In Scotland, the cask is toasted extremely superficially. It is, nevertheless, done in order to break down some of the hemicellulose into caramelized sugar. This is because heat breaks down sugar, something we are familiar with from, for example, mashing, where the unfermentable type of sugar called dextrin occurs at high temperatures. Toasting the cask also means that the lignin, the glue in the wood, is broken down into vanillin. Hopping over to the other side of the Atlantic, we can also see that the Americans have their own practices around this. A federal law from 1935 states that American distilleries must use virgin casks. In order to nevertheless tone down the effect of tannic

▲◀ A piece of an oak stave from a sherry cask used to mature whisky. Note how, on the upper side of the piece of wood, the cask contents have leached out and discolored the wood to a depth of about a quarter of an inch (a few millimeters). (Top)

acid, so called tannins, from the oak, more severe toasting is undertaken. They normally refer to four stages, with the most heavily carbonized cask referred to as "degree four," or "alligator skin" for those of you who can imagine a barbequed oak alligator.

Nowadays, maturation takes place in casks standing on loading pallets, which is obviously more practical. In older types of maturation warehouse horizontal casks are used and the design of these maturation warehouses depends on their age. As a final point, it is worth mentioning that the maturation warehouses with gravel floors, called dunnage warehouses, have acquired their name from "dunnage," blocks of wood used for stowing casks. In this context, dunnage simply refers to the wooden wedges that prevent the cask from moving. The word does not, therefore, actually have anything to do with the nature of the maturation warehouses, it refers simply to how the cask is kept in place during maturation.

The speed of the aging process depends on where in the world maturation takes place. Major differences in temperature can occur naturally and, for those producers with the necessary means, seasons can even be simulated by changing the temperatures of the maturation warehouses. At low temperatures, air is sucked into the casks and the whisky reduces somewhat in volume and, at high temperatures, the whisky expands and is forced out into the wood. The casks breathe. The vapors that evaporate as a result are called the angels' share. The extent of this also varies depending on the climate, from a low 1.5%–2% in the Orkney Islands and 2–3% in the rest of Scotland to 5–7% in Kentucky. No wonder people find the air in the Scottish countryside or Kentucky's rolling hills fresh and stimulating!

GOLD
BOWMORE

THE ORIGINAL ISLAY MALT · SINCE 1779

DISTILLED

1964

LIMITED EDITION

Good taste

Behind the whisky you like to drink, there is a whole science, or perhaps a swirling cocktail, of chemistry—esters, heavy and light alcohols, aldehydes, ketones, phenols—totaling many hundreds of flavorings in a single glass. In addition, we are talking about flavorings and aromatic substances where not even the aforementioned world of science knows everything about the interaction between the chemicals and where we don't even know everything about the origins or the identities of all the substances. We should probably be quite happy about this, since unknown factors do after all add an air of excitement to your favorite liquor and perhaps a little of that pioneering spirit when you attempt to identify the aromas.

As we know, a whisky normally contains around 40% alcohol – check! 60% water – check? No, of the remaining sixty percent a few miserable tenths of a percent consist of other substances. These fractions of the whole include various forms of sugar. There are also other substances that give the characteristic color, aroma and flavor that are typical of whisky. Certainly, a pedant would say that there is a taste to both water and ethanol and that may be the case, but that flavor profile is not characteristic of whisky in particular.

The few tenths of a percent is shared by what a puritanical chemist specializing in alcohol would call impurities. These arise or are introduced during all stages of the production process and for different reasons. Different alcohols can themselves give rise to a variety of sensations, whether this is a whiff of methanol in the early stages of distillation or the heavier alcohols towards the end. Alcohols per se may give aromas of cucumber, violets, grass and mushrooms. Through gradual oxidation, other substances are formed from the alcohols which contribute to aromas and flavors. So-called aldehydes arise when alcohol is oxidized and during the reaction is deprived of hydrogen atoms. The aldehydes arise during both distillation and the process in general. The aldehydes are often given the credit for positive experiences, such as the aroma of vanilla, cinnamon, oranges and bitter almond, and also cloves, where the substance eugenol is the active component. These pleasant aromas are derived from heavier alcohols and come from the later stages of distillation.

If the aldehydes are then oxidized a step further, acids are formed, as with ordinary ethanol which, when exposed to air, is slowly broken down into acetaldehyde, which, in turn, oxidizes into acetic acid. We're

> "If a body could just find oot the exac' proper proportion and quantity that ought to be drunk every day ... doctors and kirkyards would go oot o' fashion"
>
> James Hogg, 1826, a Scottish poet and author (1770–1835)

familiar with this from when wine or beer turns sour, and acetic acid is also found in vinegar. When reactions occur between alcohols and acids, substances called esters are formed. Esters give the whisky a fruity and even solvent-like character. The aromas from esters include apple, pear, banana and apricot as well as jasmine, rose and the more repellent smells of bug-bite ointment, nail polish and model cement. Finally, a couple of substances that deserve a place in the spotlight are ketones and terpenes. Ketones are formed when so-called secondary alcohols—where the carbon atom has a double bond—oxidize. Ketones contribute aromas that are both common and pleasant in whisky. Diacetyl is perhaps the most common, and gives a buttery fragrance. Other ketones give aromas of cheese, violet, raspberry and new-mown hay. Finally, terpenes are a group of substances used as an important component in many essential oils and perfumes. They are made up of a varying number of isoprene units and bring about aromas such as cumin, green mint, peppermint, menthol, camphor and geranium.

A bit about when the character emerges

As previously mentioned, cask maturation is the stage of the manufacturing process that provides most color, aroma and flavor to a whisky, perhaps up to seventy percent of it, even in the case of a young whisky. It is during maturation that the flavorings that perhaps most people find spontaneously and associate with whisky are introduced—butterscotch, vanilla, fruit cake, raisins, oak, nutty tones and a full-bodied, malty sweetness.

Around thirty percent of the whisky's special properties arise, however, at some other point in the production process. The raw material itself provides a malty, corn-like or rye and wheat-accented flavor depending on the type of whisky or whiskey. The characteristics of the raw liquor can be discerned even at the beginning of a whisky's production. The majority of the raw liquor's character emerges during fermentation.

For anyone who has visited a distillery, aromas associated with the raw materials, as well as pear and apple aromas, are clearly noticeable amongst the fermenting tubs at this early stage. In addition, the fruitiness of the flavor—peach, orange, apple, pear—comes about due to the way in which the yeast utilizes nitrogenous nutrients in the wash.

Of course, distillation also influences the flavor of the raw liquor and whisky. At the beginning—the head—of distillation, substances that are lighter than ethanol are separated from the low wines. The same applies to any earlier distillation, although the concentrations will then be lower. The heart is collected in the middle of the final distillation. At that point it is mainly ethanol that comes out and, depending on how high the temperature is allowed to get, a greater or lesser amount of the heavier alcohols and other substances that come towards the end are collected in

"A sweet character of burning, moist fall leaves with a certain tone of tobacco and smoked Baltic herring" or just a smoldering, fall bonfire? The pleasure of the aroma is in the nose of the beholder.

the tail of distillation. It is how generously the heart is cut, i.e., how much of the head and tail are included, that determines, along with the preceding stages in the process, the final character of the raw liquor. In the final stage of distillation—the tail—the temperature and thereby the molecular movements increase to such an extent that heavier substances are able to fight their way up through the neck of the copper still. This means that the vapors in the tail condense, run out, and contribute to both the more pleasing aromas such as the aforementioned aldehydes but also the more robust characteristics of the whisky. In the more robust corner, we recognize oiliness, smokiness and sulfurous sensations such as rubber, gunpowder and, in the worst-case scenario, musty or flesh-like smells. Although the latter are undesirable, there are nevertheless a few heavier substances that do need to be included, among them the components that smell of phenols and taste of smoke and that come at the end of distillation to give the whisky a profile of peat

smoke, phenols and perhaps the sea. Just what you want in November.

The benefit of these impurities in the distillate is that they give more character. During the many years of maturation, they will react with the cask and surrounding air. That is why the cut determines how the whisky tastes when it is ready to drink. Once maturation is finally over, the drink has been bottled and you have poured yourself a glass, it is then that aldehydes, esters, sulfurous substances and fusel oils will show their most palatable side.

The language of whisky

Every drink has its own language to describe aromas and tastes. And think about it, those of you who drink wine from time to time; blackberry jelly, toast, coffee, leather, stables and horses that have just been out running could perhaps describe a rural breakfast and a

red wine, but hardly your everyday whisky! No, for this and other drinks it is important to highlight the set of descriptive words that suit the particular drink concerned. If you do so, your analysis will not only become much easier but you will stand out among your friends as the person who can immediately work out what the whisky smells and tastes of. Obviously. Is there any whisky that doesn't have an aroma of vanilla with a suggestion of butterscotch and a certain tone of dried fruit?

Without any pretence of being scientific, there are some suggestions below of the properties to look for in order to make a tasting simpler and more fun. Aromas and flavors are divided up according to their main origins. The idea is that you should be able to draw your own conclusions, whether it is certain ages, raw materials or degrees of peat-smoke flavor you will be hunting for in order to find new favorites for your drinks cabinet.

Tastings themselves are one of the best things about whisky: sitting down in good company and letting your mind make spontaneous connections around aromas and flavors, whether you do it in an orderly manner, keeping scores and awarding points, or just after dinner for fun. Just don't take it too seriously, otherwise things could get out of control the way they did for a couple of Germans at a whisky fair recently. Both attached an almost existential seriousness to their questions. The first victim of this zealous questioning was the recognized rum and whisky author, Dave Broom, who got a telling-off as follows:

"… how long exactly is the aftertaste, in seconds? It is astonishing that you, a whisky journalist, do not know such a thing?!"

The second German bit the dust when he put a similar question to the elegant blending veteran, Richard Paterson. With his quick wit and detached irony, Paterson replied without a moment's hesitation:

"… the established view is that an aftertaste lasts for around seven seconds, although some people feel that eight is a better standard. Four to six seconds is regarded as an average-length aftertaste, while anything less than four seconds is a short aftertaste."

So there you have it. A good comeback. Unfortunately, the irony was wasted on them. The people who would benefit most from understanding irony are, as we all know, those who do not do so at all.

The transport of valuables outside Bunnahabhain.

But that said—don't let this inhibit you. This should be an unpretentious exercise. As you will have noticed, you are the only person with your nose so stick to your guns and trust the aroma you smell. Train yourself too to find more aromas and to put words to the aromas. The difficult part is not sensing the aroma, but describing it.

Allow yourself to give free rein to your imagination. There is no right and wrong. Let your thoughts float away to other things: wet dogs, model cement, fuel tablets or perhaps your favorite soft drink. An association I like to mention is that of a participant in a tasting who, like Marcel Proust, disappeared into the past as he smelled a slightly smoky whisky. With a dreamy look on his face, he quite spontaneously came out with what he could smell—an entire childhood, no less:

"It's like cap gun charges and newly-fallen dew on asphalt and perhaps a little like freshly-ironed cotton shirts ... a Bakelite telephone warmed by the sun!" was how he put it.

"Cheers and a job well done!" I said.

> "It is a statistical certainty that if you drink a glass of whisky every day for 1,200 months, you will live to a hundred."
>
> The quote, originally about cognac, from the book *Talking About Wine* by Picpoul Pinard-Poubelle.

Aromas and flavors and where they have their origins

A number of common aroma and flavor associations follow below. The table is divided into three main elements of production as a way of explaining the point at which each characteristic arises.

Aroma	Flavor, mouthfeel
Characteristics associated with the raw products and the process:	
Fresh fruit (apple, pear, lychees) Dried fruit (apricot, raisins etc.) Ripe fruit (ripe banana) Candy-like aromas (banana-flavored marshmallows, raspberry laces) Cotton candy Flowery (e.g., lilac, rose, geranium, heather) Corn, popcorn Tobacco, ozone, wax, warm cotton, cheese, musty tones	Spirity (high alcoholic content or short maturation?) Fruity sweet Malty, breadish-sweet (grain, Weetabix) Caramel, caramelized sugar Oily, creamy
Characteristics associated with peat:	
Salinity Hemp rope, ropes (sweet tarry tones) Tar, telephone pole, creosote, coal smoke, phenol Cap gun charge, sulfur Textile plaster, oilskin coat, petroleum Iodine, medicinal tones	Pepperiness Liquorice, liquorice root Cigar smoke, cigar ash
Characteristics associated with the cask and maturation:	
Oak, cedar, sandalwood Hot sauna Dill Resin Vanilla Breadish vanilla – cookie, wafer, butter biscuits Roasted tones (toasted bread, roast coffee) Butterscotch, coconut Fruitiness (pear, apple, fruit confectionary) Arrack Rubber tube (due to sherry cask of dubious quality)	Harsh, bitter, dry Like sherry, dessert wine Chocolate Nutty (walnut, hazelnut, marzipan, peanut) Vanilla Softness, lack of sharp tones

Ten of the best

Choosing the ten best types of whisky in an objective manner is impossible, as ranking them becomes a very subjective process. Nevertheless, I have made an honest attempt to include high-quality whiskies where the producer has a clear concept and high ambitions for his product. There is also some geographical spread here to provide a bit of breadth. Above all, however, this small and carefully-made selection contains a number of whiskies I recommend you try if you have not already done so. They are all available in well-stocked stores and they have also enjoyed a longer life than seasonal products, even though Balvenie Port Wood is, for me, the very definition of a Christmas whisky with its fruity, velvety body. And I can certainly state that Blanton's Straight from the Barrel is a whisky just made for the late summer—it is best drunk on warm evenings under an August moon accompanied by the clinking of ice and some good company!

Ardbeg Ten (46%)

An **aroma** of an Asian spice store, tarred hemp rope and just a hint of peppermint. In addition, a sweet, rich and, at the same time peaty aroma with elements of salt and aniseed, as if you have just opened a bag of liquorice tablets warmed by the sun. **The taste** is full-bodied and sweetly grainy. It will take on a sweeter character if you add a few drops of water. **Its aftertaste** has spicy, salty tones. Here, there is a trace of weak salmiak, a little grain husk and its long finish provides a hint of cigar smoke and burnt wood.

A young Islay whisky stored in a bourbon cask, which, thanks to its youth, has acquired malt, smokiness and also a slight full-bodiness from its ten years in an oak cask.

Balvenie Port wood, 21 year old (43%)

A **slightly acidic aroma** with flowery tones of ripe fruit with the malty, perfumish tones that are typical of Balvenie in the background. A touch of strong sweetness and also freshly baked sponge cake emerges. **The taste** has a buttery strength with traces of butter biscuit and is intensively malty with dark marmalade tones. Delicious! **The aftertaste** is intricately malty and jammy, and austere without being dry. Reminds you of the sensation you get in your mouth after swallowing a glass of a rather weak unsweetened fruit drink made from strawberries, blackcurrants and a little cherry. A little peat emerges well into the aftertaste. An excellent matured whisky that is good on its own or in company with a piece of fruity chocolate and a creamy cigar.

Matured at the neighboring Glenfiddich distillery in a bourbon cask and, finally, for 6-9 months in port pipes, i.e., used port casks with a volume of about 132 gallons (500 liters).

Blanton's Straight from the Barrel (65.3%)

The aroma is embracingly warm. Wood tones like cedar warmed by the sun and a newly heated sauna, but with a sharpness and acidity, like a freshly-chewed pencil. In the midst of this also a fine aroma combination where creamy, vanilla toffee counterbalances vigorous, crisply-burned, sugary sweetness, collectively reminiscent of well-baked, sponge cake edges. Water mellows the aroma and gives an aroma of both pear and honey. **The taste** is fierily sharp. Despite this, there is a splendid tone of arrack, overripe banana and burnt sugar in what is reminiscent of a good, dark rum, with an element of nail polish even. This quickly becomes more oaky, with the expected bourbon tones. A little water makes it more austere and gives it a more fresh oak and weak waxy honey taste. **The aftertaste** is also warm and sweet with more of a caramel tone than pure sugar. The slightly harsh oak tone moves to a hint of grain.

One of the best examples of American whiskey. Body, character and far more finesse than the packaging—with its ultra kitsch look somewhere between a hand grenade and a lamp stand. The color reveals that well-charred casks and many years in the warehouse are the foundation of this whiskey. Note too that there is a letter, one of the eight in the whiskey's name, at the rear hoof of the racehorse, so get going and start collecting!

Bunnahabhain 12 year old (46.3%)

An exciting fruity aroma with bright, warming alcohol tones and a weak but clearly peaty base. There is a feeling of creaminess here and, in addition, the often recognized aroma of freshly pulped blueberries. With a few drops of water, the sherry tones become clearer, with an ozone-like tone from the phenols. Initially it has a dark malty **taste**, not unlike the Weetabix breakfast fiber biscuits. A creamy, rich tone soon appears underneath. The heat from the alcohol is clear in the middle of the tongue and the grainy tones revel around in this fire, which soon acquires a burnt wood aroma and also a trace of ozone here. It also has a grainy character in the **aftertaste**, which passes over into a harsh but warm and crispy parting shot, with tones of slightly burnt caramelized hazelnuts.

A mild classic from Islay that, fortunately, is no longer chill-filtered and therefore retains the fine peaty tone that forms such a fine partnership with elements of blueberry and a smooth mouthfeel.

Glenmorangie Finealta (46%)

The **aroma** is a fruity, perfumey one and is oddly composed of prickly sweetness, dried fruit, some slightly peaty phenols and even a drop of nail polish. Dried fruit and vanilla dominate and the vanilla aroma is reminiscent mainly of butter biscuits. The **taste** is initially peppery, particularly if you taste another whisky from this elegant, well-tuned family in parallel. The pepperiness is joined by a creamy sweetness that has both a malty, grainy tone and also a gilt edge of phenol the whole time, just like the aroma. The **aftertaste** leads with phenols that, along with malty sweetness, are most delicious. When they fade, a soft, dry, cask tone intensifies, maintaining the theme of malty sweetness, and soon moving to a longer aftertaste of a more cereal-accented, grain husk character.

Apparently, Finealta means elegant in Gaelic. According to the producer, the recipe dates back to 1903. Here, there is a fine combination of light, smoky tones and balanced fruitiness from storage in oloroso casks. Very successful and certainly old and classic, but I become absolutely ecstatic from the first sensation in my mouth: a sensation that can only be expressed as "really good whisky" so as not to complicate matters!

Highland Park 18 year old (43%)

A **richly fruity aroma** with caramelized pears, a little dried apricot, and a touch of orange. The **taste is of unobtrusive and well-balanced sweetness** that continues to have a fruity tone with a breadish dryness that slowly releases the peat taste. The **peat tone then continues in the aftertaste**, which has light, fruity, almost perfumey, flowery characteristics that meander on towards peat and cask. Complex and uncommonly varied in the composition of its characteristics. A whisky to spoil yourself with, or else to introduce someone to the world of malt whisky with.

Forty-five percent blended in first-time cask, which makes this eighteen-year old from Scotland's most northerly whisky distillery an essential, foundation whisky for all needs; it's also, as a rule, very good value.

Lagavulin 16 year old (43%)

If you had the pockets of your oilskin coat full of fabric Band-Aids, the aroma would be like this. **Add the aroma** that comes from you swinging eighteen inches of sweet and moistly tarred rope in your hand and you get the picture. It is marine, balanced and this is not at all as ethereal as the smoky tones of Bowmore, although there is a twinge of a lighter and more perfumey peat smoke in the fleshy tarriness. The **taste** is fresh and flatteringly spirity for its age. The smokiness quickly increases and is well-preserved despite 16 years in the cask. A trace of burnt popcorn perhaps reveals that a bourbon cask has been involved. Little by little the fullness increases in the mouthfeel. **Immediately into the aftertaste, there is also a tone of woody, peppery smoke**, like chilli combined with a taste of ham smoked in elm chips. A dryness appears, and remains, while a creamy-smooth smokiness persists for a long time and develops into an increasingly sweet smokiness. An extremely good bestseller. It's nice that it's not something that could be called middle-of-the-road, not even a quarter century after it found its way into the Six Classic Malts series.

The representative for the Islay Six Classic Malts series. A surprisingly small distillery where only around ten percent of what's produced contributes, with a richly smoky character, to blended whisky.

Nikka Yoichi 10 year old (45%)

Arrack, sun-warmed oak, and acidic fruit—bitter orange and overripe oranges. There is also a very slight vanilla aroma with a slightly grassy, burnt tone. Undeniably a young liquor, but extremely well-distilled and matured. The **taste** is sweet, balanced and malty. The mouthfeel goes from smooth to fiery and has a continuing, strong, malt taste. The fullness increases towards the end. The **aftertaste** has a pleasant flavor of cask and malt. A weak bourbon-like tone is joined by a strong, dry maltiness that, in a medium-long and vegetally dry, austere aftertaste, concludes in a light vanilla and a surprising finish that becomes increasingly sweet and moves off slightly to fruit-drop with a little peat smoke.

A good representative of Japanese malt whisky. Can be recommended, despite its age, as it has already achieved a certain character at ten years of age. As a general rule, Japanese malt whisky does not reach its peak until it is eighteen–twenty years old, but it is worth the wait, I can tell you...!

Redbreast Pure Pot Still 12 years old (40%)

The **aroma** is strongly sweet and stickily fruity, prune, mashed dried apricots and a touch of ethyl acetate and oatcakes. If you add water, the ultra-sweet fruity aroma fades. It develops into a balanced, drier aroma. Interesting aromas of soft gingerbread cake and banana cake emerge and, beneath this, a weak, fleshy, phenol tone, like you sometimes find in a bitter ale. There is certainly something of the typical Irish tones of blackcurrant leaves and sauvignon blanc with bourbon accents, but these features are surprisingly weak. The **taste** is very fiery. After a few sips some honey, golden-toasted bread and warm, smooth oak emerge. Well-baked puff pastry and a touch of rum and raisin chocolate. **Aftertaste** momentarily grassily austere, developing into vanilla tones that are joined by fruit toffee aromas. The tannins give the tongue a feel of fine sandpaper. With a little water, everything is toned down and the grainy taste comes across more clearly.

This pot-still distillate is an Irish whiskey which is only a couple of years old. It also provides good evidence of how the huge increase in sales of Irish whiskey also brings with it more specialist products with elements of the original, both as a result of it being distilled in a copper still and also due to a flavor character that is considerably richer than more traditional types of whisky from the emerald isle!

Springbank 15 year old (46%)

Honey and fruit, a fresh, berry-like aroma reminiscent of cloudberry jelly and preserved strawberries in each nostril. A resilient, oaky tone that balances finely on a wave of old oaky brandy, combined with a mild tone of fresh oakwood. The **taste** is light and, at the same time, very rich. It is freshly malty, fruity and lightly acidic. Vigorous. A whiff of beeswax and honey sweetness is apparent towards the end, when a mild phenol-like peaty aroma also emerges. The **aftertaste** kicks in where the taste ends—sweet, convincing, and flowery with a fading, peaty tone. Mild toffee and weak phenol smoke. A slightly bourbonish aroma? In summary, such a complex, rich, and very well-balanced whisky that it feels over-polished. Should be on your shelf at home or in your mouth.

The showpiece brand from the distillery of the same name, which is one of Scotland's smallest distilleries. Undeniably also one of the whisky producers with the best reputation, despite its small size. Situated in Campbeltown and producing this two-and-a-half times distillate as well as the double-distilled smoky Longrow and the unsmoked, triple-distilled Hazelburn.

CLONDALKIN
BRANCH
PH. 4593311

ABC

ABV: Alcohol by volume, quite simply the percentage of alcohol contained by volume as you would expect.

Aldehydes: A group of chemical substances that, simply put, are alcohols that have lost a hydrogen atom. In one form, an aldehyde called acetaldehyde is formed when ethanol is exposed to air for a long time. It is often aldehydes that are referred to when a whisky has the aroma of different flowers. Other well-known aromas with aldehydes as their base are the aromas of nutmeg, cinnamon (*cinnamaldehyde*), vanilla (*vanillin*), bitter almond (*benzaldehyde*) —i.e., Amaretto liqueur!

Amylase: A group of enzymes that break down starch. As far as whisky is concerned, they are referred to in mashing where they are found in the barley and break down the starch into fermentable types of sugar.

Angels' share: The share of maturing whisky that evaporates from the cask. It's called this because it is all the angels get. On the other hand, it is duty-free and represents 2–3% per year of all the whisky matured in Scotland; it is more than double this in Kentucky and perhaps half this in chilly Sweden.

Arrack: Originally a distillate from, among other things, sugarcane juice. The distillate has a typical aroma that can often be recognized in liquor that has been matured a long time. The arrack aroma in matured liquor is directly related to fusel oils and is often found in matured fruity liquor that contains a lot of heavier alcohols after distillation. The aroma is sometimes found in whisky and even more often in grape distillate and, above all, in dark rum.

Barley: The variety of grain that, due to its very existence and the fortunate fact that it contains a mixture of useful elements, has proved excellent for the production of alcoholic grain-based drinks—a high starch content and plenty of enzymes that can break down the starch into fermentable sugar. The most common are two and six-row barley, with the two-row variety being used in whisky production.

Barrel: A barrel in general, but also, more specifically, whiskey barrels from the USA, which contain around 50 gallons (180 liters).

Blended whisky: Whisky blended from rectified spirits, grain whisky and single malt whisky. Typical proportions are 30% malt whisky of twenty or so different kinds and the remainder grain whisky.

BPS: British Plain Spirit, raw liquor from the still. This term is often used as an explanation of what is referred to in statistics as produced volume in liters.

Butt: Name for barrel size, usually around 132 gallons (500 liters) but may vary from 129 gallons (491 liters) up to 168 gallons (636 liters). Originally a type of sherry barrel.

Column still, continuous still, patent still: Column still, also called Coffey still after its inventor, the former Irish excise official, Aeneas Coffey.

Cut: The extent to which the raw liquor is collected, determined by the kind of character the producer wants the distillate in the final still to have. A broad cut means that both lighter and heavier substances are included before and after the ethanol, while a narrow cut means that a meager portion of the heart of the distillation is collected so as to achieve a purer and more neutral spirit.

Dextrin: Unfermentable, simple type of sugar that arises when starch is broken down by high levels of heat. Compare with the brown bits on buns; this is actually dextrin that is created in the heat of the oven.

Diastase: One of the enzymes that contribute to breaking up the starch into fermentable sugar types, e.g., to malt sugar.

Draff: The remains of the malt that are left once the wort is filtered out. Remains at the bottom of the mash tun and is used as animal feed.

Dreg: Generally sludgy sediment, in particular the fine sediment that gathers at the bottom of the mash tun, in a distillation column, or at the bottom of a barrel.

Esters: A group of chemical compounds that are formed when an acid reacts with an alcohol and, with a surplus of water, forms a fragrant ester. Another type of ester is the waxes that are formed if a fatty acid with a long carbon chain reacts with an alcohol. If the alcohol is glycerol, the result will also be a fat. Esters have, among other things, fruit aromas and can also be used as solvents. Typical ester aromas are apple (the ester *pentyl pentanoate*), pear (*pentyl butanoate*), the scent of roses (*geraniol*) and also ethyl acetate, which can be recognized as the smell of adhesive or nail polish.

Eugenol: Pronounced *yew-jin-all*. The fragrance in cloves. It is a superior alcohol with a strong bactericidal effect. It has also been used in dental care for disinfection. For this reason, it's an aroma that many elderly people associate with less positive memories of the dentist. In whisky, the aroma may derive from substances that have their origins in oakwood and also in raw liquor.

Feints: The tail of distillation, i.e., the part of the distillation that goes to be redistilled because it contains too much of the heavier alcohols.

First fill cask: A term meaning that the raw whisky is put in a cask that is being filled for the first time with whisky after having previously contained, say, bourbon or sherry.

Fusel oils: A generic name for heavier alcohols that are treated mockingly and unfairly. This is despite the fact that, along with their little siblings in the head of the distillation, they are one of the prerequisites for an eventful maturation that brings out many aromas (Also known as: *fusel alcohols*)

Geraniol: The fragrance that gives, for example, the rose geranium plant (*Pelargonium graveolens*), also called the rose-scent geranium, its typically sharp, fresh, stimulating, almost peppermint-like aroma.

Grain whisky: A whisky produced in a column still, with greater purity and fewer flavoring substances.

Green malt: Barley that has germinated after having been moistened during the steeping process. As a result of kilning—the roasting of the green malt—it loses its prefix and, once dried, becomes simply "malt".

Head: The first of the three parts of the final distillation. Evaporates up through the neck of the still at the beginning of distillation, i.e., when heated. The head contains, therefore, lighter substances such as aldehydes and esters with their flowery and fruity aromas, but also methanol, for that matter. Like fusel oils, these are, to a certain extent, desirable for giving the whisky development potential during maturation.

Heart/cut: *Coeur* in French. The middle point of the second distillation. Usually collected at a strength of between 72–73% and down to 67–68% alcohol.

Hogshead: Name of cask size, usually 66 gallons (250 liters), but exceptionally up to 73 gallons (275 liters).

Ketones: Chemical compounds that are responsible for several of the aromas in whisky that most fire the imagination. Diacetyl, the substance that provides a cheesy aroma, belongs to this group of compounds. Other aromas that have ketones as their source are the aroma of raspberry (ionone), violet, and also hay and newly-mown grass.

Kiln: The building in which the germinating green malt is roasted to stop it germinating. In principle, the building is a furnace with a fine-meshed grating where heat, and often also peat smoke, filter up through the green malt to roast it and sometimes add taste. The kiln often has the characteristic pagoda-like roof that is typical of whisky distilleries.

Lomond still: A hybrid of the column still and the pot still, constructed with the idea of collecting different types of raw liquor by varying the degree of distillation in the same still.

Lyne arm: The tapering end of the copper stills that malt whisky is distilled in, resembling a swan's neck.

Malt whisky: Whisky made from only barley malt, yeast and water and distilled in pot stills. It is a single malt if it comes from only one distillery.

Mash bill: The recipe that specifies the apportionment and choice of the three or more ingredients in American whiskey.

Mashing: The stage in the process where warm water causes the barley's enzymes to break down the starch into fermentable sugar.

Oak: Type of wood that is very suitable for making casks for maturing beverages. There are about 600 species, only a few of which are suitable for making barrels for drinks. The oak gives the beverage tannic acid—tannins—and in so doing provides a balance to the sweetness of the whisky and tightens up, strengthens and complements the properties of the content of the barrel. The most common species for maturing whisky are the European sessile oak, *Quercus petraea*, and the common oak, *Quercus robur*, and, in the USA, *Quercus alba*, the white oak, which gives less taste and color. The latter gives a less complex taste, a paler color and a distinctly austere wood character combined with marked vanilla.

Peat: Partially-decayed vegetation that, when burned, gives a varying, smoky aroma, depending on the types of plant the peat originates from.

Pint: A well-known British beer measurement that is, more precisely, 20 fluid ounces, or 0.5678 liters, or 2 cups!

Pipe: Name of a particular cask size, usually around 132 gallons (500 liters) and with its origin in maturation casks for port, often referred to as port pipes.

Pot ale: The remains of the wash after distillation, also called burnt ale.

Pot still: The name for the covered pot that enables a steaming, distilling wash or low wines to be distilled into a liquid containing even stronger alcohol.

Reflux: The term for how much of what is condensed inside the whisky still runs back, and can thereby be redistilled while the current distillation is ongoing. The greater the reflux the lighter and purer the raw liquor.

Rummager: A mechanism equipped with arms with chains that slowly rotates inside coal-fired whisky stills so that the liquid does not burn and stick to the bottom.

Slàinte: Cheers in Gaelic. Pronounced, roughly, "schlanjay". Often heard loudly and slurred in many languages other than Gaelic. "To your very good health" is "Slàinte mhòr agad!", which should be pronounced roughly as schlanjay vore agg-udd! You often see the simpler "Slàinte math!", which translates as "Good Health", with the second word pronounced "va!"

Spent lees: The dregs in the distillation still.

Spirit safe: The aquarium-like, and generally well-polished, brass and glass box that makes it possible for the liquor to be cut within a closed environment. Initially introduced in connection with the changes in the law in 1823. First tested at the Port Ellen distillery and invented by a Mr Septimus Fox.

Steeping: The first stage in malting where the barley is given a real soaking; it is normally soaked three times and drained, and begins to germinate immediately afterwards.

Tails: The stage of the final distillation that takes place when the heat has increased in the still to the extent that heavier substances slip up through the swan neck to be redistilled. This includes, for example, what we call fusel oils.

Tannin: The same as tannic acid. Found in relatively abundant quantities in oak, which benefits the cask content of both Rioja wines and malt whisky. Also found in, for example, spruce, which is how the acids acquired their name, as spruce bark was historically used in the tanning of leather.

Terpenes: This group of chemical compounds includes fragrances that provide aromas including crude rubber, cumin (*carvon*), menthol, and camphor (*camphan*).

Uisge beatha: Gaelic for "water of life". Note that the word whisky comes from an anglification of the Gaelic for water.

Vanillin: An aldehyde with an aroma that is one of the aromas the human sense of smell finds easiest to recognize in small concentrations. The vanillin comes partly from eugenol in the raw whisky and partly from oak. The vanillin from oak is a result of the breaking down of the glue—lignin—in the oak wood that happens when the inside of the cask is toasted or burnt. In chemical terms, vanillin is an aldehyde, closely related to the fragrances in nutmeg and cloves.

Vatted whisky: Whisky blended from different types of single malt. Nowadays also called blended malt. Comes from the word *vat*, a cask.

Wash: A wort that has had yeast added until it has finished fermenting and is ready to be distilled. Usually has an alcohol content of 7–9%.

Wash still: Also called a low wine still. The first of the two stills the Scots generally use for distilling.

Wood finish: Finishing off maturation by changing the cask to something sweeter, fruitier or just more pronounced, as is done, for example, at Glenmorangie as Sauternes, port and sherry maturations and Balvenie, with both distinct sherry and bourbon maturations and also a smooth port finish. The finish, which generally uses first fill casks, lasts between six months and a couple of years. If it is done well, it strikes a good balance with the character of the whisky which should be evident in the interplay with the final maturation, the latter being the icing on the cake of a good basic maturation.

Wort: The sugar solution, mainly containing water and malt sugar, that results from mashing.

Yeast: A single-cell fungus that has a pleasing effect on sugar—carbon dioxide and ethanol. Its magical effect was a secret until the middle of the 19th century when Emil Christian Hansen, among others, discovered at Carlsberg in 1883 that the amazing magic was simply the result of a controllable fungus that could be cultivated and developed in the desired direction.

References

Books, articles:

AFLODAL, Henrik. 2008. *Whisky, Japan*. Balkong Förlag.

BARNARD, Alfred. 2000. *The Whisky Distilleries of the United Kingdom*. First published 1887, facsimile edition Rasch Edition, 2000.

BILLER, Peter & HUDSON, Anne (ed.). 1994. *Heresy and literacy, 1000–1530*. Cambridge University Press.

BROOM, Dave. 2009. *The art of science*. Whisky Magazine 84/2009.

BROOM, Dave and Rob ALLANSON. 2009. *Japanese oak*. Whisky Magazine 84/2009.

BUXRUD, Ulf. 2007. *Michael Jackson*. Svenska Dagbladet, 14 September 2007.

BUXRUD, Ulf. 2008. *Japanese whisky—facts, figures and taste*. Dataanalys Scandinavia.

CAMPBELL, Humphyn. 1834. *Selection of reports and papers of the House of Commons..., vol. 13: Select committee on sale of corn"*, 17 January 1834.

COFFEY, T. M. 1975. *The long thirst—prohibition in America: 1920–1933*. WW Norton & Co.

CURTIS, Wayne. 2006. *And a bottle of rum: a history of the New World in ten cocktails*. Crown Publishers.

DEARY, Terry. 1998. *Horrible Histories, Bloody Scotland*. Scholastic Children's Books.

DELOS, Gilbert. 1996. *All världens whisky [The whiskies of the world]*. Wahlströms.

ELLSBERGER, Per. 2007. *Skotsk whisky, allt om maltwhisky [Scotch whisky, everything you need to know about malt whisky]*. Prisma.

GUSTAFSSON, Bengt Y (ed.). 1976. *Atlas till historien [Historical atlas]*. Esselte Studium.

HIBBS, Dixie. 2002. *Bardstown: Hospitality, history and bourbon*. Arcadia Publishing.

HOFFMANN, Marc A. 2008. *Whisky från hela världen [Whisky from all over the world]"*, Tukan Förlag/Parragon Books Ltd.

JACKSON, Michael. 1989. *Michael Jackson's Malt Whisky Companion*. Dorling Kindersley.

JACKSON, Michael. 1999. *Michael Jackson's Malt Whisky Companion*. Dorling Kindersley.

JACKSON, Michael. 2005. *Whisky*. Dorling Kindersley Ltd,

KRASS, Peter. 2004. *Blood & whiskey, the life and times of Jack Daniel*. John Wiley & Sons.

LANGLEY, Andrew. 2001. *Timeless spirit*. Irish Distillers through Good Books Publishing Ltd.

LYNCH, Michael. 1992. *Scotland, a new history*. Pimlico.

MACLEAN, Charles. 2004. *MacLean's miscellany of whisky*. Little Books Ltd.

MCDOWALL, R.J.S. 1986. *Whiskies of Scotland*. New Amsterdam Books/Meredith Press.

MCGUIRE, Edward B. 1973. *Irish Whiskey: A History of Distilling, the Spirit Trade and Excise Controls in Ireland*. Gill & Macmillan.

MURRAY, Jim. 1998. *Classic bourbon, Tennessee and rye whiskey*. Prion Books Ltd.

MURRAY, Jim. 1997. *Jim Murray's complete book of whisky*. Carlton Books Ltd.

MURRAY, Jim. 2005. *Jim Murray's Whisky Bible 2006*. Carlton Books Ltd.

MURRAY, Jim. 2009. *Jim Murray om Michael Jackson— fullständigt briljant [Jim Murray on Michael Jackson—absolutely brilliant]*. Allt om whisky magazine, 1/2009.

NILSSON, Hasse. 2011. *Två i fokus [Two in focus]*. Whisky & Bourbon, 3/2011.

O'HART, John. 1999. *Irish pedigrees, or the origin and stem of the Irish nation, vol 1*. Genealogical Publishing Co, Baltimore, USA (Reprint 1999). First edition J Duffy, Dublin, 1892.

QUINN, Tom. 2005. *The whisky companion*. Think Publishing.

RALPH, Ron. *Production of American whiskies: bourbon, corn, rye, and Tennessee.From: PEARSE LYONS T. et al (ed.). 2003. The alcohol textbook*. Nottingham University Press, fourth edition.

RAY, Cyril. 1977. *Alla dessa drycker [All these drinks]*. Wezäta Förlag.

RIEGLER, Susan. 2001. *Kentucky*. Fodor's Travel Publications.

RONDE, Ingvar (ed.). 2011. *Malt Whisky Yearbook 2012*. MagDig Media Ltd.

ROSKROW, Dominic. 2009. *But Mr Ambassador ....* Whisky Magazine, 82/2009.

ROSS, James. 1970. *Whisky*. Routledge.

SMITH, Gavin D. 1997. *A to Z of whisky*. Neil Wilson Publishing Ltd, (1993).

SMITH, Gavin D. 2009. *Northern highland highlights*. Whisky Magazine, 77/2009.

STANDAGE, Tom. 2005. *A history of the world in 6 glasses*. Walker Publishing Company.

STIRK, David I. 2005. *The Distilleries of Campbeltown: The Rise and Fall of the Whisky Capital of the World*. Neil Wilson Publishing.

TEELING, John. 2008. *The Renaissance of Irish Whiskey*. Cooley Distillery, 16 April 2008.

THURFJELL, Karsten. 2012. *Maltwhisky—en global angelägenhet [Malt whisky—a global affair]*. Bolaget, no 3 September 2012.

WESTRIN, Th. (ed.). 1909. *Nordisk Familjebok [Nordic Family Book]*, 10th volume; Gossler–Harris, Nordiskt Familjeboks Förlags AB.

WIZNIEWSKI, Ian. 2009. *Rising to the challenge*. Whisky Magazine, 83/2009.

Internet:

(the date given is the date when the information at the link provided was read, unless otherwise stated)

BUNTING, Chris. April 2011. *Nonjatta* (a blog about Japanese whisky). Available at: nonjatta.blogspot.com

CLARKE, Jim. Published April 2004, read 2012. *An interview with John Teeling of the Cooley Distillery, Ireland.*

At: www.starchefs.com/wine/features/html/cooley_distillery_interview.shtml

COLLINS, Michael. July 2011. *Did You Know? 19th Century Cognac History.* At: www.brandyclassics.com

JOHNSTON, T B; F.R.G.S. & ROBERTSON, J.A. *Historical Geography of the Clans of Scotland, The Disarming Act 1746, 19 Geo. II c. 39.*

At: www.scotgenealogy.com/webclans/geog/chapter10.htm

KRAAIJEVELD, Alex. May 2012. *The birth of the pagoda roof.* Celtic Malts. At: celticmalts.com

LUDING. April 2012. *Calvet, France.* At: www.luding.ru/en/suppliers/france/ calvet/

Merriam-Webster Dictionary. February 2012. At: www.merriam-webster.com/ dictionary/gauge

PUTZ, Jean-Marie. December 2011. *History of Scotch whisky between 1788–1823.* At: www.whisky-distilleries.info

SMITH, Gavin D. March 2012. *Twelve dates of whisky.* At: www.lfw.co.uk/ whisky_review/SWR12/article12-5.html

STEVENSON, Sandy. January 2012. *Scottish whisky.* At: www.fife.50megs.com/scottish-distilleries.htm

Forbes. October 2011. At: www.electricscotland.com

The Information about Ireland Site. 2000. At: www.ireland-information.com

Distilled Spirits Council of the United States. 2011. *Prohibition Fast Facts.* At: prohibitionrepeal.com/history/fastfacts.asp,

Alastair. February 2012. *Lindores Abbey—Home of Scotch whisky.* At: www.thewhiskybarrel.com/blog/post/id/56/n/lindores-abbey.

Other:

Interview in December 2011 with Paul Kendall, archivist at William Grant & Sons.

Interview in October 2011 with Barry Crockett, master distiller at Midleton Distillery.

Interview in April 2007 with Ian Williams, distillery manager at Cardhu.

Thanks

To my dear family, who have patiently allowed me some kind of peace and quiet to work, even though it's a strain on everyone's patience when what is called work seems to have to happen at the oddest of times, and also constantly. If I could, I would hug you from morning to night!

But that will have to wait until this book is finished, won't it?

Folke Andersson: for his help on the history of whisky in Sweden.

Roger Brashears, Jack Daniel's: for truths and tall stories about both whiskey in general and Jack Daniel's in particular.

Andrea Cagliesi: for frosty February pictures of Scotland—and for entrusting me with the first whisky tastings at Mackinlay's, many, many years ago!

Barry Crockett and **Liam C O'Leary**: for the history of Irish whiskey in general and Midleton in particular.

Angela D'Orazio, Mackmyra: for a hospitable tour of Mackmyra's facilities both overground and underground.

David Francis, William Grant & Sons: for excellent photographic opportunities, information and contacts.

Paul Kendall, archivist at William Grant & Sons: for history and material about William Grant.

Caroline Låftman, Philipson & Söderberg: for illustrations.

Martin Markvardsen, brand ambassador Edrington Group: for instant help with history.

Roger Melander, Box Destilleri: for an exhaustive tour with both tasting and tapping.

Chris Morris, Labrot & Graham: for insights into whiskey production and his great generosity as a host.

Micke Nilsson, Akkurat: thanks for accompanying me on my travels and also for inputting your skills in the Japanese language.

Fred Noe III, Jim Beam: for a warm and hospitable reception at both the maturation warehouse and on the porch.

Heléne Reuterwall-Thideman, Pernod Ricard Sweden: for illustrations and establishing contacts in Ireland.

© for the original edition:
Stevali Production and Örjan Westerlund

Original title:
Whisky, whiskey & bourbon

Photographs by the author, except for the following sources of illustrations:
Portrait of the author by Micke Nilsson.
Andrea Cagliesi: pages 22–25, 33, 133.
Diageo: page 45.
Edrington Group: page 77
Nikka: page 101.
Pernod Ricard Sweden: pages 31, 70–74, 126 bottom right.
Philipson & Söderberg: pages 10–11, 18, 38–39, 50, 52, 87, 90 100, 102–107, 128 top right,
132 top right and bottom, 138, 140, 156–157, 172.
Spirit of Hven: pages 124 top picture, 128 bottom right picture, 130.
William Grant & Sons: pages 13, 14, 44, 49, 51, 79, 118 bottom picture, 122 top picture.
Bottles pages 146–150: pictures from respective producers.
Map on page 54 by Stevali Production

Graphic design and production: Alan Maranik/Stevali Production
Copy-editing: Benny Eronson

© for the English edition:
h.f.ullmann publishing GmbH
Special edition

Translation from Swedish: Edwina Simpson in association with First Edition Translations Ltd, Cambridge, UK
Editing and typesetting: First Edition Translations Ltd, Cambridge, UK
Project management for h.f.ullmann: Isabel Weiler
Cover design: Simone Sticker
Overall responsibility for production: h.f.ullmann publishing GmbH, Potsdam, Germany

Printed in China, 2013

ISBN 978-3-8480-0408-9

10 9 8 7 6 5 4 3 2 1
X XI VIII VII VI V IV III II I

www.ullmann-publishing.com
newsletter@ullmann-publishing.com